D1545045

The Too Hot To Cook Book

A WILLIAM COLE BOOK

WALKER AND COMPANY

New York

THE TOO HOT
TO COOK BOOK

MIRIAM UNGERER

ILLUSTRATED BY
TOMI UNGERER

Contents

For Pamela
> *Who spent her allowance on artichokes*

For Shelly
> *For whom the end of the meal*
> *is the beginning*

For Phoebe
> *Hooked on straight noodles at the*
> *age of three*

Introduction

Summer cooking does not necessarily mean to me that everything should be in aspic or turned out of a can at a moment's notice. It does mean taking advantage of the particular gastronomic pleasures of the season. Fresh vegetables and fish are rarely better than when uncluttered by a lot of time-consuming side dishes. The French and Italian custom of serving new asparagus or baby string beans as separate courses makes a little event out of food that we usually treat in a routine manner.

Actually fresh garden peas and unfrozen spring chicken may be nearing extinction. In the knowledge that we are possibly the last generation to know the true flavor of foods that have not been mechanically tampered with, we should savor the fleeting flavors of summer eating to the fullest.

This book is for people who delight in rediscovering the remembered fragrance of last summer's strawberries, the salty tang of freshly dug clams, or half a summer's flavors cooked in a ratatouille. Even though the canner and freezer have made asparagus in December and Brussels sprouts in July utterly commonplace, they do not replace fresh vegetables ripened at leisure and served in their own time and place.

Some of us will spend the summer at the shore or in the mountains; others will be pounding the city pavements for all but a few weeks. There are dishes for those with the time and inclination to indulge their food fancies, and there are recipes for people who enjoy eating but don't really wish to make a big production out of it.

Quite a number of rather fancy-sounding dishes are made very quickly. Sauce Parisienne for poached or baked fish is an elegant touch; it is the base of a number of other derivative sauces, and takes only about 10 minutes to produce. Steak au Poivre flambé takes about the same amount of time. Even the celebrated Bouillabaisse with its rather frightening number of ingredients is only a fish stew with a lot of lovely flavors boiled rapidly together in about 30 minutes. Advocates of advance cooking are really safer with winter stews and cassoulets. But the informality of summer entertaining and the gregarious aspect of the hibachi and outdoor grill make last-minute cooking less of a bore and a chore.

Summer is the time of the clambake and the picnic, as simple or elaborate as you choose. One stop at a good Italian food shop can provision you with a spicy hard salami, some salty thin sheets of prosciutto, a loaf of good bread and freshly made mozzarella, white and dripping with whey. You need only a bottle of wine and wheels to find a special place to enjoy your outdoor feast. For others, there is nothing like a good exhausting afternoon digging a pit for a clambake and starting the long-smoldering fire, scrubbing clams, soaking the corn and organizing the ritual feast.

Delicate chilled soups and airy mousses are elegant summer specialties to tempt the most jaded palate. But that is seldom a problem during vacation days. There are rather the monstrous appetites whetted by clean fresh country air and the relaxation that affords time to dwell on the pleasures of summer and of summer eating. I hope this book will add to both.

introduction

Stocking a Summer Cupboard

Primarily this concerns seashore or country vacation houses, since otherwise you can just dash right out and get what you need or forget the whole business and go out for dinner. A sophisticated array of foods and condiments in the grocery stores does not happen to be one of the charms of most of the resort villages and towns. Clerks have looked askance at a request for whole peppercorns and totally blank at an inquiry about saffron in the seashore community where we summer. Good cooking doesn't require a lot of exotic things but it is nice to be able to extend a last-minute invitation to dinner and to produce something a little more than routine.

With a couple of cans of kidney beans, some good olive oil, garlic, onions and lemons you can produce a main course salad for 8 nearly immediately. Canned chicken and beef stock simplify the preparation of summer soups and risottos. A variety of pastas: cavatelli, fusilli, farfalle, or green noodles in addition to the usual spaghetti and linguini are all delicious with simple, quickly made sauces of fresh herbs and tomatoes or just butter and garlic with some cheese freshly grated from your store of Parmesan or Romano.

These are some other useful things to stock the vacation-house cupboard with:

whole peppercorns
saffron
fine quality curry powder
cumin (seeds or powder)
Hungarian rose paprika
olive oil
peanut oil for deep-frying
canned tuna fish, anchovies, white kidney beans, red kidney beans, Italian plum tomatoes, tomato paste, liver pâté, garbanzos, nuts, chicken stock, beef bouillon, tomato juice, dry oil-cured olives, ripe olives, green olives, pimentoes, artichoke hearts, palm hearts, imported wild mushrooms such as those called "chanterelles" in French and "pfifferlinge" in German, smoked baby clams or oysters
dried leek and mushroom soups
capers
hot Dijon-type mustard and dry mustard
converted rice and wild rice
several kinds of pasta

piece of Romano or Parmesan cheese (refrigerated)
unflavored gelatin
smoked sausages and a bacon square (refrigerated)
wine vinegar and tarragon vinegar
Madeira wine
dry Port
an assortment of dry white wines and red wines for drinking
   and cooking
cognac
kirsch
bottled mineral waters
beer
unsweetened crackers in tin boxes
sweet cookies in tin boxes
piecrust mix
jar of shelled, blanched almonds
nonperishable chocolate (a new instant-mix type that comes
   in plastic packages)
extra-fine granulated sugar (for fruit compotes)
dried herbs, if you cannot get fresh ones
espresso coffee and special aromatic blends of tea, if you   7
   like them.

    These are for consideration to add to your basic stores
and all are long-lasting if not absolutely nonperishable.
    Besides chanterelles, imported cheeses, kirsch and Earl
Grey tea, which one cannot expect to find in every village
store, there are some other limitations to cooking in a
vacation house. The equipment in a rented kitchen: the thin,

stocking a summer cupboard

battered, tin skillet, worn-out saucepan with the handle that turns, and the dime-store "stainless steel" knife with the tip broken off. This is not to mention the stove, which probably saw its finest hours during the Coolidge Administration.

If cooking and eating are any part at all of your summer enjoyment, do take along a few competent pieces of kitchen equipment and spare yourself needless frustration. In a cast iron skillet with a cover, food can be sautéed, roasted, baked, broiled, boiled or braised. One decent all-purpose steel knife for chopping and carving, a vegetable peeler and the type of can opener you can operate safely will save a great deal of irritation and maybe a finger. A wooden spoon, a wire whisk and a food mill will enable you to make creamy sauces, puréed soups or a superb mayonnaise. A cheap oven thermometer will help you to adjust to the crotchets of your stove and keep your hostessing gracious.

If there are no pots capacious enough for cooking corn, shellfish and soups or pasta for at least eight people, it is annoying to try to cook these things in several batches. You can always use an 8-quart heavy aluminum pot to pack the other kitchen things in; it makes a rather striking piece of luggage.

Herbs

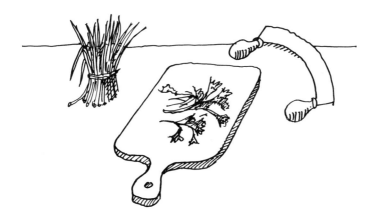

Dried herbs, no matter how fine the quality, can never compare with fresh ones. Summer's special gift to the cook is an array of fresh herbs. You can grow them in pots in a sunny city window, in a small country garden (even a weekend gardener can manage herbs), or buy them in farmers' markets and vegetable stands. Unfortunately, I have yet to see a supermarket, even at the height of season, that goes in for anything more exotic than parsley. But we may count that not too small a blessing since parsley is probably the most versatile and useful herb there is.

Tarragon, sweet basil, bay leaf, thyme, marjoram, chives, summer savory, rosemary and dill weed are, along with parsley, the most popular cooking herbs. Except for rosemary, which tends to drop dead if a draft hits it, all of them are easy to grow. You may purchase small plants from a nursery or order them by mail.

I have omitted sage from my list because I think its taste overwhelms almost any food, and oregano because I ate in too many cheap Italian restaurants many years ago.

Fresh herbs will keep for a couple of weeks in the refrigerator if they are left unwashed and stored, loosely separated, in air-tight plastic containers. Moisture and tight packing of the leaves rot the herbs.

Even if you set out only one of each herb you wish to grow, there will undoubtedly be a delightful surplus which you should by all means dry for winter use. If you do the very simple operation properly, your herbs will certainly surpass any commercially dried product. Parsley and chives do not dry very successfully, but anyway, parsley is always available and frozen chives aren't bad.

To dry herbs, leave the sprigs as intact as possible. The leaves will retain their flavor longer if dried on the stems. With cotton string, tie the stem ends together in small bunches and hang upside down in a dark, dry closet. Or lay out in a single layer on newspapers, cover with cheesecloth and another sheet of newspaper and dry them out slowly at 140° F. or the lowest heat your oven can maintain. After about half an hour, turn off the oven and leave the herbs overnight. The leaves should be dry but not crumbling to powder. Store the herbs in labeled opaque or dark-colored glass jars with tight stoppers. Light deteriorates the flavor of herbs, which may be why commercial brands of dried herbs often taste as if they've been cremated rather than dried.

Herbs dried hanging up may take a couple of weeks, but I think they are much more aromatic than artificially dried herbs. When using dried herbs remember that the concentrated taste of them requires only one fourth the amount of fresh herbs you would use. Of course, in the case of some brands, you could use the whole jar without altering the character of the dish in the least. Always test any dried herb by crushing a tiny bit in the palm of your hand. If there is not an immediate pungent response, throw the bottle out. Either omit the herb from your recipe or select a suitable alternate. Any herbs more than a year old should be thrown away.

Hors d'oeuvres

Since informality is indigenous to summer entertaining, it seems really pretentious to struggle with fussy hors d'oeuvres all gussied up in coats of aspic. Anyway, Saran Wrap has mercifully taken over the role of aspic, which was invented to preserve the moisture and flavor of food.

I confess that I am not very enthusiastic about this category of food in summer except to serve at parties. I dislike having my guests sit down to dinner stuffed with stuffed eggs and potato chips. However, cocktail parties, no matter how informal, do demand some thought, if not too much effort. I find that a large amount of two or three things, rather than an infinite variety of tids and tads, is easier to manage. A whole corned brisket of beef requires no attention at all as it simmers slowly on the back of the stove. Served up with horseradish and mustards and rye bread, this makes fine fare with almost any drink. Cold roast lamb or veal are more interesting alternatives to the omnipresent ham stabbed with pineapple-laden toothpicks.

Summer is the time to take advantage of some of the delicacies that can be bought ready to serve: smoked salmon, trout, eel, butterfish, sturgeon and whitefish. These need only a choice of good breads, some lemons, capers and onions to make a superb and effortless display of party food. Letting the guests choose and build their own hors d'oeuvres solves two problems: the time you spend in the kitchen and the preservation of the freshness of the food. Fancy canapés require a staff of at least two: one expert in the kitchen and a waitress. Since the object of having a party is to have a good time with your friends, cook ahead or stick to simple things.

SMOKED FISH

Smoked Nova Scotia salmon, sturgeon and whitefish are always available in New York's fabulous delicatessens. Gourmet food departments of big stores provide these things in most cities. If your summer is spent on the shore, investigate the local smoked fish. On the eastern end of Long Island, eel is inexpensive and abundant in the summer.

Smoked butterfish are occasionally around. Smoked trout from England and salmon from Scotland are no bargains in price but are an incomparable way to splurge once in a while.

Eel, butterfish and trout must be skinned before serving and cut into pieces not more than 2 inches long. Slice some rye, pumpernickel and white toast into pieces that match the size of the fish slices. Serve a small bowl of capers, some lemon wedges, thin slices of onion and provide a pepper mill.

Good smoked salmon is neither greasy nor particularly salty. It is rather dryish and the slices tend to stick together. Since it is expensive and difficult to separate, it is the one thing that should be cut up and arranged on thinly buttered slices of bread in advance. It may be covered with Saran Wrap and refrigerated until serving time.

15

hors d'eouvres

SHRIMP RAVIGOTE

Allow 1½ pounds of shrimp for 4 people.

Cooking shrimp is so easy that it's ridiculous to pay the extra price for precooked shrimp of heaven knows what age and condition. However, cleaning shrimp is a great bore. Train your children early to do this job efficiently. Those plier-like shrimp cleaners in hardware stores do not work. Medium-sized shrimp are best for this dish. Rinse quickly and cook them, unshelled, in Court Bouillon (see recipe). They are done when they turn pink; usually in 3 to 5 minutes. Drain them and clean as follows:

Pull off the legs all at once with your thumb, forefinger and middle finger. Usually, the shell will slip off easily in one piece. Starting where the head was detached, grasp the tip of the back intestinal vein and strip it down the back. It breaks sometimes and you will need a small paring knife to get out the bits of sand. On no account wash the shrimp after it is cooked; its flavor is elusive enough as it is.

Place the shrimp in an earthenware or china bowl and add some small, mild white onions sliced very thin. Pour on some Sauce Ravigote (recipe follows), cover and refrigerate for 4 or 5 hours. Garnish with tomato wedges or little cherry tomatoes and serve as a first course or a main luncheon dish.

SHRIMP WITH AÏOLI

Allow 1½ pounds of shrimp for 4 people.

Cook and clean the shrimp as for Shrimp Ravigote. Aïoli is a Provençal garlic mayonnaise, delicious on shrimp as well as on raw vegetables (see recipe for Aïoli). Arrange the shrimp on a large round platter with a bowl of Aïoli in the center. *Variations:* Serve the shrimp with Sauce Rémoulade or Green Mayonnaise instead of Aïoli.

SAUCE RAVIGOTE

Few cookbooks agree on what this really is. Many recipes are almost identical to Sauce Rémoulade, but this version does not contain any mayonnaise. In any case it is usually served on cold meats, fish or vegetables, and is one of those thrifty French ways to dress up yesterday's dinner for today's luncheon.

1 cup Sauce Vinaigrette (see recipe)
2 or 3 Tb minced fresh herbs such as parsley, chives, chervil, tarragon, marjoram or thyme
2 tsp finely minced scallions
1 tsp chopped capers
3 or 4 chopped anchovy fillets (except when sauce will be used with chicken)

Shake all ingredients together in a screw-top jar. Do not use a blender, as it destroys the individual textures and flavors.

SHRIMP BAGNA CAUDA

Bagna Cauda means "hot bath" and is an Italian sauce served with raw vegetables as an antipasto. This sauce must be kept hot over a small flame while it is served.

Cook and clean the shrimp. Refrigerate in a tightly closed plastic bag until serving time. Provide small skewers or toothpicks and serve with this sauce:

2 cloves garlic   ¾ cup olive oil
¼ lb butter   ¼ tsp crushed red pepper
5 anchovy fillets, minced   OR/a few drops of
2 tsp fresh basil, chopped   Tabasco sauce

Mince the garlic and add it to the butter. Melt the butter, taking care that it does not brown at all. Beat in remaining ingredients with a wooden spoon. Serve very hot but not hot enough to fry the shrimp, as it is a sauce, not a cooking agent. *Variation:* If you wish to augment the shrimp supply, add some sliced raw mushrooms or some slivers of green peppers.

hors d'eouvres

SHRIMP MARINATED WITH DILL

serves 6-12

Poach the shrimp in Court Bouillon (see recipe) and shell it. As an hors d'oeuvre, 2 pounds of shrimp will serve 6 people. If it is only one of several hors d'oeuvres platters for a party, 2 pounds will probably be all right for 12.

2 lbs medium shrimp, cooked	*1 cup olive oil*
	½ cup dry white wine
1 cup finely chopped fresh dill weed	*1 tsp mustard powder*
	½ tsp salt
½ cup minced scallions	

In a narrow, deep, glass or china dish, alternate layers of shrimp and dill weed. The container should be filled to the top. Beat the salt, mustard and white wine together, then slowly beat in the olive oil. Pour this dressing over the shrimp and dill, cover and refrigerate for 8 hours. Stir the mixture up twice during this time. At serving time, drain, sprinkle with chopped scallions and mix lightly. The shrimp may be served on a small plate as a first course or on a large platter with toothpicks for spearing.

CHINESE SHRIMP TOAST

This must be assembled quickly and at the last minute. It is so delicious that only a firm refusal to go on frying and frying will save you from missing your own party. Allow 2 pieces per person, but a lot of people will try to get 3 or 4.

*½ lb cleaned, minced raw
    shrimp
6 water chestnuts, chopped
1 tsp salt
pinch of sugar
1 tsp minced fresh ginger
    (or ½ tsp powdered)
2 Tb scallions, chopped*

*1 Tb sherry
1 egg, well beaten
peanut or corn oil
1 Tb cornstarch
6 slices home-style white
    bread, 2 days old (or
    spread out to dry during
    the day)*

Combine all ingredients except cornstarch and bread. Mix well. Add the cornstarch and allow to stand while you trim the crusts and slice the bread diagonally into two triangles.* Spread a heaping tablespoon of the shrimp mixture onto each triangle. Deep fry 3 or 4 pieces at a time, face down, in 1 inch of very hot peanut or corn oil about 3 minutes, or until golden. Turn and fry briefly on the other side. Drain on absorbent paper and serve absolutely immediately.
*Note: The recipe may be prepared in advance up to this point. No matter how dubious the procedure sounds, the shrimp will NOT fall off the toast while frying.

19

MOULES MARINIÈRE

Mussels are not much appreciated by Americans and consequently are very cheap in the few markets that carry them. They are one of the most succulent and easily prepared of all shellfish. The fact that you can gather all you want for nothing on Northeastern beaches outweighs the somewhat tiresome cleaning process. In some markets mussels are sold by the pound and in others, by the quart. Allow at least 1 pint of mussels in the shell per person. Allow more if your guests have decent appetites. Mussels must always be cooked prior to using them in any recipe. This is the basic method of preparation:

1 qt large mussels	*6 to 8 peppercorns*
1 cup dry white wine	*1 clove garlic, split*
1 onion, chopped	*2 sprigs parsley*
½ bay leaf	*French bread*

Scrub the mussels under cold running water with a stiff brush until they are shining clean. Holding the mussel in your left hand, use an ordinary table knife to pry out the "beard"—the small, mossy growth it uses to cling to its rock bed. It isn't necessary to scrape off any barnacles except for esthetic reasons. Put the wine, onion, bay leaf, peppercorns, garlic and parsley into a large shallow kettle with a cover. Put in the mussels, preferably not more than two deep. Bring to a boil, then lower heat. After about 2 minutes of steaming, stir the top layer of mussels down to the bottom so that they will cook evenly. Continue steaming until all the mussels are open. This should take no more than 5 minutes. *Do not overcook* or they will be rubbery, tasteless and nearly invisible. Do not attempt to pry open any mussels that have not succumbed to the steaming. They are either shells full of mud, or defective in some way and should be tossed out.

Using the lid to hold the mussels in the pot, strain the juices through cheesecloth laid in a strainer to catch the sand which the mussels have released. You will now have 3 or 4 times as much liquid as you started with. Bring the wine and juices to a boil again and add 1 tablespoon of softened butter into which you have worked as much flour as it will absorb. Stir it vigorously into the broth to thicken it a little. Taste for salt and pepper. Put about a dozen mussels in a shallow soup plate with a chunk of toasted French bread. Pour the soup over all, sprinkle with a bit of fresh, chopped parsley and serve very hot. This dish is usually served as a main course. It is given here to indicate cooking directions for the following recipes.

MOULES RÉMOULADE

Steam the mussels as for Moules Marinière but do not bother to thicken the soup. You may strain the liquid and save it to cook other fish or shellfish. Allow 6 mussels per guest. Drain the mussels and remove the top shell. Arrange them on a bed of romaine or lettuce and squeeze a few drops of lemon juice on each one. Cover with Saran Wrap and chill. When you are ready to serve, put about 1 teaspoon of Sauce Rémoulade (see recipe), depending on the size of the mussel, on top of each mussel.

MOULES VINAIGRETTE

Prepare as for Moules Rémoulade substituting a well-flavored Sauce Vinaigrette (see recipe). The mussels are often removed from their shells entirely and presented in small ramekins. It doesn't really matter but forks should be provided as this is too messy for finger eating.

hors d'eouvres

SPICED CORNED BEEF

Corned brisket of beef may be bought at almost any supermarket in the meat department. It requires long, slow simmering but no finesse whatsoever. Try to get a lean piece; the firmer the meat, the leaner it is.

3 - 4 lb corned brisket of beef (cross cut)	1 Tb fresh thyme OR/½ tsp dried thyme
1 onion stuck with 3 cloves	1 bay leaf
2 cloves garlic	1 tsp cracked black pepper

water to cover

Wipe meat with paper toweling. Place in a heavy pot with a cover and add all other ingredients. Add NO salt. Slowly bring to a boil, skim, reduce heat to barely simmering for about 3 hours. Adjust the lid slightly askew. Water level should be maintained at about 1 inch above the meat. Pierce with a fork to test for doneness. Don't cook it too long or it will fall to shreds when carved.

Allow the meat to cool in the broth. It will still be warm after 2 hours and it absorbs more flavor during this time. Let the meat rest on a carving board about 10 minutes, then slice it ⅛-inch thick.

The corned beef should be served tepid with a cold sauce made of sour cream or fresh whipped cream to which you have added fresh horseradish to taste. Serve with pumpernickel or rye bread.

CURRIED MEATBALLS

If you have no way to keep these really red hot, don't bother with them. Tepid, tasteless meatballs are a specialty of catered affairs and certainly no one strives for that effect. This mixture also makes an excellent meatloaf.

1 lb ground lean chuck beef	pinch of allspice
½ lb ground veal	1 tsp pepper
½ lb ground pork shoulder	½ tsp thyme
2 eggs, beaten	1 clove garlic, minced
½ cup minced onions	3 cups beef bouillon
2 Tb butter	curry powder to taste
½ cup cognac	(1 Tb or more)
1½ tsp salt	2 Tb cornstarch dissolved in a little cold water
	salad oil

Sauté the onions in the butter and add to the 3 ground meats in a large bowl. Mix well. Beat in the eggs with a wooden spoon. Add salt, pepper, allspice, thyme, garlic and cognac. Form a small ball and fry it so that you may taste it and adjust seasonings if necessary.

Form meatballs about the size of a walnut. Coat a heavy skillet with plain salad oil and sauté the meatballs for about 5 minutes, shaking the pan often to brown them evenly and retain their round shape. Sauté a single layer at a time and do not crowd them. When all are done, pour off any fat and deglaze the pan with ½ cup of bouillon. Stir in 1 tablespoon of good curry powder and add remaining bouillon. Bring to a boil and slowly add the cornstarch dissolved in water until the sauce is as thick as medium cream. You may not need all of the cornstarch. Add more curry powder if desired. Place the meatballs in a chafing dish and pour the curry sauce over them. They should simmer in the sauce a while and do not seem to be harmed by a fairly long wait.

hors d'oeuvres

PÂTÉ MAISON TOBY

Most French chefs will reward you with a frigid stare should you ask for their pâté recipe. This one was given graciously by an American friend and will tie for honors with the best you can find in the French countryside. No real pâté de campagne is quick and neither is this one. But pâté is so excellent a summer dish, it is worth the effort for a special occasion. Also, this recipe will serve about 25 people or it can be brought out from the refrigerator numerous times over a couple of weeks.

1 lb fresh pork fat, sliced very thin	¼ cup heavy cream
	½ cup cognac
1 lb boneless pork	3 eggs
1 lb boneless veal	4½ tsp salt
1 lb ham steak	2½ tsp white pepper
½ lb pork or chicken liver	½ tsp thyme
10 cloves garlic	½ tsp allspice
½ cup flour	

Fresh, not salted, pork fat is essential. (If you haven't got a meat grinder, have the butcher grind all the meats separately except the pork fat and liver. These may be minced finely with a sharp knife.) Grind ¼ pound of the pork fat with all the veal and pork using the fine blade of the meat grinder. Set aside. Line a 3-quart mold (or you may use 3 aluminum-foil loaf pans—in this case you will need 2 pounds of pork fat for lining them) with the thinly sliced pork fat, starting at the center and letting the long ends of the strips hang over the sides of the mold. Grind the ham and remaining pork fat with the coarse blade of the grinder. In an electric blender, purée the liver with the garlic, cream, cognac and eggs. (If you don't own a blender, mince the liver and beat the mixture up by hand.) Gradually add to the blender mixture ⅓ of the ground pork and veal mixture. In a large bowl combine the blender mixture with all the ground meats. Beat in remaining seasonings and flour with a wooden spoon. Fill the prepared mold with the pâté mixture and fold the overhanging ends of pork fat over the top. Cover the pâté air-tight with a double thickness of aluminum foil and place the mold cover on top of that. Set the mold in a pan of water half the depth of the mold and bake it in a 400° F. oven for 3 hours. Remove cover and foil and bake 15 minutes longer to brown the top. Leave the mold in its underpan and remove it to a place where it can rest undisturbed until it is cool. Replace the foil and weight the pâté by placing a plate or pan that will fit just inside the mold directly on top of the foil. Fill the top pan with canned goods or other objects weighing about three pounds. When the pâté has cooled completely, store it covered in the refrigerator. It will keep for about 2 weeks.

Note: Some people advise freezing pâté but I think it's a catastrophe; the texture is ruined by sogginess caused by thawing.

SMOKED SLICED TONGUE

Some smoked tongue can be bought ready-cooked, but for a crowd it is more economical, and very simple, to cook your own. Soak a 4- or 5-pound smoked beef tongue in water a few hours, or as long as overnight. Simmer it according to the directions for Spiced Corned Beef with these substitutions: Omit the garlic and add half a lemon. The meat will probably need from 3 to 4 hours of gentle simmering. When tender, remove carefully (this is easier if, before cooking, you wrap the tongue in a long double layer of cheesecloth and let the ends hang out over the top of the pot), skin, and remove any small bones or membranes at the base of the tongue. Serve at room temperature or chilled. Always slice tongue diagonally and as thinly as possible. A flaming hot mustard or horseradish sauce is usually served. A Sauce Ravigote (see recipe) is good with this dish if you wish to serve it for a luncheon main course.

hors d'oeuvres

VEGETABLES à LA GRECQUE

Mushrooms are most commonly served in this style. However, artichoke hearts, celery, cauliflower, fresh asparagus tips, young carrots or any fairly firm young vegetables you choose can also be prepared "à la Grecque." Any raw vegetable should be cut into bite-size pieces and parboiled. It is not wise to mix the vegetables before they are cooked because some of them would be overcooked. Each different vegetable should retain its own special flavor and texture. Mushrooms should first be sautéed quickly, rather than parboiled.

½ cup olive oil
juice of 3 lemons
½ tsp salt
1 cup water
6 coriander seeds, 12 peppercorns, sprig of thyme, bay leaf, and 2 sprigs of parsley tied in a cheesecloth bag

Combine all ingredients and bring to a boil. Add one of the suggested vegetables and enough boiling water to barely cover. Reduce heat and simmer until just tender. Drain vegetable, reserving the marinade. Boil rapidly to reduce the marinade to about 1 cup. Put the cooked vegetables in a tall, narrow jar and pour the cooled marinade over them. Chill in the refrigerator 24 hours if possible.

STUFFED MUSHROOMS

Although the really stupendous mushrooms—sometimes 3 or 4 inches across—are rarely available except in autumn, good cultured mushrooms are available the year round. You must pick out the freshest, large white ones for stuffing. This dish is quite rich and may also be used for a luncheon main course for 4 persons.

16 large mushrooms	salt and pepper
¼ lb mushrooms, any size	pinch of nutmeg
½ cup thick white sauce (Béchamel)	grated Romano or Parmesan cheese
¼ cup white onion, minced	½ lb butter
¼ cup parsley, minced	½ cup minced cooked chicken or veal (optional)

Unless the mushrooms are particularly sandy, just wipe them carefully with damp paper towels. Detach the stems and cut off about ⅛ inch from the tough end. Wash, dry and mince the ¼ pound of mushrooms along with the stems from the large caps. Melt 3 tablespoons butter in a heavy skillet and sauté the caps lightly. Remove to a baking dish, cavity side up. In the same skillet, melt 4 tablespoons butter and add the minced mushrooms. Stir over medium heat until they have cooked quite dry. Stir in the minced onion and cook until softened. Off heat, stir in the white sauce, nutmeg, parsley and season carefully with salt and pepper. Add cooked chicken or veal, if desired.

Fill the sautéed mushroom caps with the mixture. Sprinkle with grated cheese and bake in the upper third of a preheated 375° F. oven until the caps are tender and the stuffing has browned. This should take about 20 minutes. *Note:* Instead of the white sauce, you may use 3 or 4 tablespoons of fresh white breadcrumbs mixed with 4 tablespoons of heavy cream. A tablespoon of Madeira or dry Port may be added.

EGGPLANT PURÉE

serves 10-12

Eggplant is a gorgeous vegetable with an unfortunate name. Perhaps if we changed it to the French, *aubergine*, it would be served more often. Near and Middle Eastern recipes use its delicate flavor in a variety of ways and this is one of them.

2 medium eggplants	½ green chili pepper,
1 clove garlic (or more)	minced
¼ cup olive oil	juice of ½ lemon
6 scallions, minced	salt and pepper

Grill the whole eggplants until they are tender and the skins begin to blacken slightly. The faint burnt flavor that the skins impart to the flesh contributes to the impression that you have created the dish hunched over 4 smoldering bits of charcoal. Peel them, chop them roughly and put them in a food mill or an electric blender. Purée the eggplant with the garlic and olive oil. Turn into a bowl and add the scallions, green chili pepper and lemon juice. Add salt and pepper to taste. Mix well. The garlic, scallions and lemon juice must all be adjusted to taste. Garnish with Greek olives and serve with bread or unsalted chowder crackers. If you can find some "flat bread" in the special shops that cater to Middle Eastern customers, that would be ideal.

No Cooking Things

In addition to the smoked fish, excellent gooseliver-style liverwurst, sausages and cold cuts that are ready to serve when you get them home, there are some other ways to avoid the stove.

FISH ROES

Lumpfish roe looks something like caviar and is quite tasty even though it does leave you with a sooty smile. Red caviar is becoming more popular and is easily obtained in most localities. Serve it mixed with sour cream as a dip. Pressed caviar is relatively inexpensive, but is rather sticky. It can be improved by mixing it with lemon juice and a little oil.

Fresh fish roe, such as shad, is excellent poached, then mashed with lemon juice, raw onion juice and a little olive oil. Beluga caviar is, of course, the ultimate solution for an hors d'oeuvre. Serve it in the jar on a bed of ice with lemon wedges and hot, buttered toast.

SARDINES

Those lovely, plump skinless and boneless sardines from Portugal served right in the can are one of my favorite snacks. Arranged on a plate with some lemon wedges, thin slices of onion and hot toast they are a quite respectable offering at cocktail time. Sardines should always be part of an antipasto arrangement with the usual salami, artichoke hearts, pimentoes, etc. Hard-cooked eggs and sardines seem to hit it off together and a lusty sardine and onion sandwich will be liked by most men.

QUICK PÂTÉ DE FOIE

Only one brand of liver pâté that I know of can be recommended for this delicious deception and that is Sell's. The finished mixture should be packed into an attractive little terrine or soufflé dish.

> 4 Tb softened sweet butter
> 2 cans Sell's liver pâté
> ½ small mild onion
> 2 tsp cognac
> black pepper

Cream the butter and liver pâté together with a wooden spoon. Grate the onion into the mixture using the finest holes on the grater. Mix. Add cognac and pepper and mix thoroughly. Pack into a mold, cover and chill for at least one hour. Serve with hot toast or unsalted crackers. No one is going to think this is foie gras, but they won't know what it really is either.

TUNA FISH PÂTÉ

Five or ten minutes is all that's needed to get this together and it will keep in the refrigerator for a couple of
days if you just want to have something on hand.

> *1 can best-quality tuna fish, drained*
> *3 Tb sweet butter, softened*
> *½ tsp lemon juice*
> *black pepper*

Pound the tuna fish or put it into an electric blender with the
butter until the mixture is a smooth paste. Add the lemon
juice and pepper to taste. Pack it into a small mold and chill
until needed. Serve with capers and toast.

MARINATED SCALLOPS

serves 4

Many clam and oyster fanciers are appalled at the
thought of scallops in their natural state. But they are
delicious raw, the flesh made somewhat more firm-textured
by a lime juice marinade.

> *1 lb sea scallops*
> *juice of 4 or 5 limes*
> *Sauce Vinaigrette*

Sea scallops should be cut into halves or quarters so that the
pieces are about 1 inch across. Drain them, rinse with cold
water and put them in a deep bowl with lime juice to cover.
Marinate for 3 or 4 hours in the refrigerator. At serving time
drain the scallops and serve them on a bed of lettuce and
cucumbers. Pass a bowl of Sauce Vinaigrette (see recipe).
This recipe serves four amply as a first course. Larger quantities are fine for parties and are convenient to eat with
toothpicks.

hors d'eouvres

MELON OR AVOCADO
WITH PROSCIUTTO

Since melons and summer are made for each other, it's a fine time to take advantage of the local crop. Chilled cantaloupe and honeydew both present a luscious taste and texture contrast to thin, salty slices of Italian ham. The blandness of the avocado is an excellent background to the spiciness of the ham. Smithfield ham may be served the same way. For individual servings, slice the melon in wedges and drape with 2 or 3 slices of prosciutto. For parties, cut the melon in cubes; wrap each one in a strip of ham and fasten it with a toothpick.

FRESH RAW VEGETABLES

Garden fresh vegetables are becoming so rare it is a pity to cook them. Our home-grown American custom of eating raw vegetables is even spreading to France where it was once regarded as barbaric. "Les Crudités" are replacing those ghastly "Hors d'Oeuvres Variés" platters scattered with odd bits of yesterday's vegetables. Deploring this rare misfortune of French thrift, the great chef Carême said "Leftovers must be employed with caution, ability and, above all, silence."

Tiny crisp string beans, baby carrots, very young cucumbers, white and red radishes, spring scallions, cauliflower buds, young, tender asparagus tips and freshly sliced mushrooms make a garden-fresh appetizer. Coarse salt, butter and a garlic mayonnaise are all the embellishments needed. Or serve your own favorite dip or mine, which is Tapenade.

TAPENADE

Raw vegetables are delicious served with this rich, piquant and rather ugly gray-green sauce. It is very good with breadsticks too.

1 Tb capers	*black pepper*
8 anchovy fillets	*1 tsp lemon juice*
½ cup olive oil	*1 clove garlic*
1 can tuna fish	*raw onion, grated*
	(optional)

Mash the capers, tuna and anchovy fillets thoroughly and blend with the olive oil. Add black pepper, garlic and lemon juice. A bit of raw onion grated in is nice if you like a little added bite to the sauce. It is quick and simple to make in a blender.

RAW SHELLFISH

Clams, the proletarian oyster, are a cheap and plentiful alternate to oysters in many areas. To serve them at home they should first be scrubbed and chilled for several hours. Allow 6 clams per person. Gently pick one up. (Stuart, my favorite Long Island fish dealer, says the clams get nervous and clam up if you jiggle them.) Insert the clam knife quickly near the point of the triangularly shaped shell and pry up. Slide the knife around the outer edge without mangling the clam inside and remove the top half of the shell. Open the clams over a bowl so that if you slip and lose the juice you can put it back. Lay each clam half on a prepared bed of crushed ice. (The fish dealer will usually sell you some.) Opening clams is a man's job because even Little Necks can be very stubborn. If you just can't get anyone to open them, the fish dealer will do it for you; the clams should be rushed home and served within an hour. Lemon juice is the best accompaniment but you may serve a spicy horseradish and tomato sauce if you prefer.

Soups

Summer soups are generally shivering things piled in perfect porcelain and apparently designed to be admired rather than eaten. There are a few cold soups that I find tasty as well as attractive, but for jellied soups you will have to look elsewhere. Personally, I think a good, hearty fish or clam chowder or a freshly brewed blend of summer vegetables is a very fine thing to eat on a summer evening. There are within living memory of almost everyone I know numerous damp summer weekends spent peering out at unremitting rain squalls. At such a dreary time, start a soup and get out the poker chips.

SORREL SOUP

serves 4-6

This soup announces that summer has arrived in France. Sorrel, so frequently used in French cooking, is an alien in the United States. Still you may find some at a European vegetable market or grow it in your own garden. Canned sorrel is available in food specialty shops.

> *¼ lb fresh sorrel*
> *2 Tb butter*
> *2 cups chicken broth*
> *1 egg yolk*
> *1 cup heavy cream*

Shred the sorrel and wash it thoroughly. Wilt it in the butter, put in the chicken broth and heat to boiling point. Beat the egg yolk with the cream and beat a little of the hot soup into the mixture. Then beat the egg-cream into the hot soup with a wire whisk. Reheat and serve hot or chill in the refrigerator and serve ice cold.

Note: This soup can also be made with Swiss chard, young spinach or watercress, all of which taste different from sorrel, but very good nevertheless.

EASY FISH CHOWDER

serves 6-8

Since I discovered a dried leek soup of Swiss manufacture, I have used it as the well-flavored base of fish or clam chowder. If you do not have it on hand, make a white roux in the soup kettle after sautéing your bacon and onions and proceed with the recipe.

¼ lb smoked bacon
2 onions, chopped
1 pkg dehydrated cream
   of leek soup
1 cup dry white wine
1 8 oz bottle clam juice
1 qt boiling water

2 cups potatoes, peeled
   and diced
2 lbs fish fillets, firm fleshed
   and ½-inch thick OR 2 lbs
   frozen haddock or cod
½ pint fresh cream
4 Tb fresh parsley, chopped

salt and pepper

Cut the bacon into small cubes (or cut it into small pieces if it is sliced bacon) and try it out in a heavy skillet or soup kettle. Remove and set aside for later use. Cook the onions in the rendered fat until softened but not browned. Stir in the dried leek soup mix (or 3 tablespoons of flour) and cook, stirring for a few minutes. Add the wine, clam juice and boiling water while stirring constantly. When soup begins to thicken, half cover and simmer for 10 minutes. Add the potatoes and cook for 20 minutes. Cut the fish into bite-size (not itsy bitsy) pieces and add it to the chowder. Simmer 10 minutes, then stir in the cream and parsley and heat through for a minute, but do not boil. Season to taste with salt and pepper. Serve in flat soup plates sprinkled with some of the crumbled bacon reserved at the beginning of the recipe. Corn bread and a salad make a meal sublime.

MUSSEL SOUP

serves 8-10

Alexandre Dumas was a noted gourmet and cook who devoted both his culinary skill and literary talent to his aphoristic *Le Grand Dictionnaire de Cuisine,* published posthumously in 1873. Like those of most good cooks, his methods were old-fashioned even in his time. But his knowledge of food and cookery was so sound that his recipes are translatable into modern recipes in many instances. Dumas' soup required 8 hours for preparation but you may begin about an hour before dinnertime.

12 white onions	*salt and pepper*
12 tomatoes	*1 clove garlic*
2 qts beef bouillon (canned	*1 Tb olive oil*
bouillon will do)	*3 qts mussels (in the shell)*

French bread (optional)

Chop the onions and tomatoes coarsely and simmer them in the beef bouillon for an hour. Extract the seeds and pulp by passing the soup through a food mill or by pulverizing in an electric blender. Put onion and tomato mixture back into a pot and simmer, uncovered. Scrub the mussels and put them in another pot with a few tablespoons of water to steam open, which should take about 5 minutes. Shell the mussels and strain their juice through cheesecloth. Add the juice to the tomato and onions. Crush a clove of garlic and cook it lightly in the olive oil. Put in the shelled mussels and swirl them around in the garlicky olive oil, then pour them into the soup. Serve with plain French bread for sopping and mopping.

CLAM CHOWDER

This is made in exactly the same way as fish chowder except that 3 or 4 cups of chopped chowder clams are substituted for the fish. Someone once advised me to chop the clams in an electric blender. Don't. It makes a slimy, aerated mess of them. Get the fish dealer to open the clams, reserving their liquid. At home, chop them finely with a large heavy knife and pour their liquid into the soup along with the bottled clam juice. Do not add the clams until a few minutes before serving the soup or they may resemble boiled rubber bands.

GAZPACHO I

serves 4

Spanish cooking has contributed little to the health or pleasure of the world's gourmets but it has saved the face of many a noncook with this one dish. It is made in about as many different ways as there are Spaniards and it is enjoyed by nearly everyone. This version is a cross between a salad and a soup.

¼ cup olive oil
8 saltines, crushed to
   powder
2 cups tomato juice
1 cup beef bouillon

2 medium onions, minced
1 green pepper, minced
2 cloves garlic, crushed
juice of 1 lemon
dash of Tabasco
1 cucumber

Mix oil and saltines together, then add remaining ingredients except cucumber and chill for at least 2 hours. Soak the whole cucumber, peeled, in ice water for 1 hour before serving time. Slice it paper thin and stir it into the soup just before serving.
Note: If there is too much soup, you can reserve part of it for the following day *before* adding the cucumber. Do not refrigerate in a metal container.

GAZPACHO II

serves 6-8

This puréed version was given me by a French chef who of course swore it was the only *true* Gazpacho. He felt that using an electric blender robbed the soup of its delicate texture but, unless you have the galley staff of a Madrid hotel on hand, I think the small sacrifice is worth the saving in labor.

⅓ cup olive oil
1 cup tomato or V-8 juice
1½ cups water
10 sprigs watercress
juice of 1 lemon
2 ripe tomatoes
2 green bell peppers
bit of hot red pepper or a
few drops of Tabasco
sauce

2 cloves garlic
1 small onion, chopped
1 cucumber
salt to taste
1 cup heavy cream
8 scallions, minced very
fine

In an electric blender, purée all ingredients except the cream and scallions. Strain through cheesecloth into a nonmetallic container and refrigerate for at least 2 hours. Just before serving, stir in the heavy cream with a wire whisk. Garnish the soup with the minced scallions and serve in chilled bowls.

40

CUCUMBER SOUP

serves 8

The frequency with which this soup is served by anyone in possession of an electric blender has slightly blunted its considerable charm. However, no summer soup chapter could be complete without at least one cucumber recipe. Cucumber soup is elegant, easy and inexpensive to make for a large number of people. It tastes good even if drunk out of paper cups at a picnic.

4 Tb butter	1 cup watercress leaves
½ cup scallions	salt and freshly ground
3 cups chopped, unpeeled	black pepper
cucumber	1 cup heavy cream
¾ cup diced potatoes	1 cup milk
4 cups chicken broth	minced chives or chervil

Heat the butter and wilt the scallions in it. Add the cucumber, potatoes and chicken broth and simmer together 15 minutes. During the last 5 minutes of cooking, add the watercress leaves. They impart a sharp tang and pleasant green color to the soup. Salt and pepper to taste. Purée in a blender, then stir in the cream and milk. Chill for 2 hours in a nonmetallic container. Garnish the soup with minced chives or chervil or a mixture of both herbs.

GARDEN SOUP

serves 10

There is no better moment to enjoy a garden-fresh vegetable soup than when the makings are at their peak of flavor. Unlike a rich, slow simmered winter soup, hearty and filling with turnips and cabbage, a summer blend should be lightly cooked and each vegetable retain its freshness, flavor and texture. Prescribing exactly what to put in a vegetable soup would be a bit like a numbered canvas that the artist could never claim as his own. This is a rough outline to fill in with your own design. This serves 10 to 12 as a main course.

2 qts water
salt
2 cups baby carrots, sliced
2 cups new potatoes, diced
2 cups peeled ripe
   tomatoes, diced
2 cups scallions, sliced
1 cup fresh green lima
   beans

1 cup fresh tiny green
   beans, cut in 1-inch
   lengths
1 cup fresh okra, sliced
1 cup fresh corn, scraped
   off the cob
1½ cups cooked rice

Salt the water lightly and bring it to a boil. Add the carrots, potatoes, tomatoes, scallions and lima beans and boil gently for 30 minutes. Add the green beans, okra and corn and simmer for about 15 minutes longer. Place a spoonful of cooked white rice in the center of each soup plate and ladle some hot soup over it. Pass a bowl of Provençal Sauce, Pistou, for each diner to stir into his soup.

PISTOU

4 cloves garlic
¼ cup fresh basil, chopped
2 Tb fresh parsley, chopped
½ cup olive oil

3 Tb tomato paste
½ cup grated Romano
   cheese

In a mortar, pound the garlic to a paste with the basil and parsley; add the tomato paste and cheese. Beat in the oil by droplets, then beat in 1 cup of hot soup. Pour the sauce into a small bowl and pass it around with the soup.

ITALIAN HEBREW SOUP

serves 6

This borscht was eaten by an Italian food writer in the home of a Livornese Jewish family. He came away ecstatic and recommended it to all his friends, "baptized Christians, circumcized Moslems, idolaters or fire-worshippers." This is from *Il Gastronomo Educato* by Alberto Denti di Pirajno.

½ lb cooked beets (fresh or canned)
1½ qts salted water
1 Tb vinegar
3 eggs
salt and pepper
12 small potatoes

Simmer the beets in the salted water and vinegar for 20 minutes. Pass through a sieve (or purée in an electric blender). Beat the eggs briskly in a large bowl and pour into the beet broth, beating all the time. Season with salt and pepper and chill. Serve ice cold and give each guest a small bowl of hot boiled potatoes that have been swirled in butter or goose fat. Eat a little potato with each spoonful of soup.

ICED CHICKEN SOUP

serves 6

A first-rate Sunday brunch course, this light, delicate soup is soothing, healing and simple to make.

3 cans clear chicken stock (the kind you do not dilute with
water)
1 Tb fresh tarragon, minced
¼ cup fresh parsley, minced
1 cup heavy cream

Bring chicken stock to the boiling point and blanch tarragon and parsley. Remove from heat, stir in the cream thoroughly and chill for 2 hours. The soup should be quite thin and light textured. Serve it in large chilled china or glass cups.

SPRING PEA SOUP

serves 6

Every dish on the menu can't be a cold one without boring everyone to tears no matter how warm the weather may be. This is a delicate hot soup that anticipates a refreshing chilled main course.

1 Tb butter
1 cup diced potatoes
3 cups chicken broth
1 cup freshly shelled green peas
1 Tb chopped chives

Melt the butter in a soup pot and swirl the potatoes around in it. Add the chicken broth and simmer until the potatoes are soft, about 20 minutes. Purée in a blender and return soup to the pot. Bring to a boil and put in the fresh green peas. Cook them until just tender (test by eating one) and stir in the chopped chives just before serving.

Salads

Salads are the most abundant and appropriate mainstays of summer meal-planning. However, no course is treated in a more monotonous manner by Americans, who are generally thought to be fanatic salad eaters.

Many quite competent cooks profess to be mystified by a simple oil and vinegar dressing. Then there are the High Priests of the Salad Bowl—usually men who have learned to officiate at a Caesar Salad. Somewhere between the two extremes lies the making of a dew-fresh green salad, glistening in a light dressing, and fragrant with the season's herbs.

One divine ritual of no value at all is the anointing of the salad bowl with a sliver of garlic. Some garlic-hater must have thought up that effete practice. Another notion that must be dispelled is that all the preparation of an excellent, crisp salad must be done in a last minute frenzy. It is, however, absolute Gospel that you cannot add other ingredients or dressing to the greens until the moment before serving. It is also preferable not to tear the greens, much less *cut* them (heinous!) until just before dressing them.

Those who have been resigned to serving a bowl of exhausted salad greens reclining listlessly in an acrid bath of oil and vinegar usually are victims of only two small, but fatal, mistakes: too much vinegar and too little drying of the greens. Therefore, we will start with basic training on that indispensable complement to a summer meal, Plain Green Salad.

PLAIN GREEN SALAD

It is best not to wash salad greens if you have to keep them any length of time. Water starts to rot the leaves when they are pre-washed and enclosed in a plastic bag in the refrigerator. Generally, salad greens should be used as quickly as possible after purchase or picking.

Wash the salad thoroughly, separating the leaves. Invert in a colander to drain. Detach, shake and pat the leaves dry between paper toweling. Store, rolled loosely jelly-roll fashion, in a slightly damp dish towel for up to 2 hours in the refrigerator. Some slightly wilted greens will crisp up nicely in an *open* plastic bag in the refrigerator.

Prepare a Sauce Vinaigrette, which is what French Dressing really is. That pink, sticky banality we've all come to know and loathe as "French Dressing" is a purely American invention. The sheer density of it is enough to beat a tender little lettuce leaf into submission, to say nothing of smothering its delicate flavor.

VARIOUS SALAD GREENS

In the summer months the varieties are particularly large and appealing and leave no excuse for choosing that horror, iceberg lettuce, so aptly named for its flavor.

Alternate and delicious choices are:

BOSTON LETTUCE, also known as butter lettuce. This soft-leaved pale-green lettuce with a rather crisp, pale-yellow heart is becoming quite popular in the northeast United States and usually can be found in markets throughout the country. It has an extremely subtle flavor that is quickly dissipated by refrigeration. It is best to store it in a cool, dark place wrapped in damp paper towels or newspapers. If you are fortunate enough to have a kitchen garden, pick it (like any other greens) as late as you can before serving. Most tender salad greens should be spared refrigeration except for possibly an hour or so to chill the prepared leaves.

BIBB LETTUCE, sometimes known as Leaf lettuce, has quite delicate, tender leaves that bruise easily. Usually home-grown or bought at country roadside markets.

SALAD BOWL, a large, bushy lettuce with tender, curly leaves, is a fairly recent, prize-winning development. Rapidly becoming more common in city markets because of its popularity, it is also called Australian or Oak Leaf lettuce.

ROMAINE, available everywhere because of its travel hardiness, suffers the drawback of having a somewhat tough, fibrous texture. The spine of the larger leaves should be ripped out. Its spicy brittleness is interesting mixed with other greens and it is excellent "bedding" for mayonnaise and meat or fish salads since its large, strong leaves do not wilt readily.

CHICORY, also called curly endive, has the characteristic slightly bitter flavor of the endive family. Its leaves are sharply feathered and somewhat resemble Salad Bowl, but are much crisper. An entire salad of this green would be unpleasant to most people, but it adds a nice piquancy and texture to the softer salads.

BELGIAN ENDIVE, also called Winter or French endive, is a pale yellow to white tight cluster of slender, pointed leaves, shaped something like a small banana. Its waxy, crisp texture and slightly acrid taste are best enhanced by a plain French Dressing with a dash of mustard. Belgian endive, along with what we call Boston lettuce, are the most frequently served in France. It is mystifyingly expensive, since it ships well. Now available the year around, although more plentiful in winter.

WATERCRESS has real personality. Unlike any other salad, its dark-green, spicy, petal-shaped leaves have a distinctive pungent flavor that always seems to be best with a lemon and oil dressing and an extra dash of fresh black pepper. Watercress, which until lately shared the fate of parsley—chiefly to garnish steak and chops—makes a delicious salad all by itself or in combination with other milder-flavored salad greens.

SPINACH makes an unusual addition to a mixed green salad. Only the small, dark, glossy leaves of very young spinach will do for salad. It is really supreme in counterpoint to fresh, sliced white raw mushrooms, the two textures and flavors dressed with a good Sauce Vinaigrette.

CALVES TONGUES, also called field salad; dandelion greens, alias Pissenlits; fiddlehead ferns and nasturtium leaves are for esoteric tastes and likely to stay so since they are so difficult to obtain. They are quite good for one-upping food snobs if you really want to go out of your way.

ESCAROLE, with its tough, leathery leaves, and *iceberg lettuce* are last resorts and I would rather eat cole slaw.

salads

FRENCH DRESSING OR
SAUCE VINAIGRETTE

Measure into a small dry screw-top jar:

3 Tb good olive oil
½ to 1 Tb wine vinegar or 1
  Tb lemon juice
⅛ tsp salt

freshly ground black pepper
¼ tsp dry mustard
  (optional)
mashed clove garlic
  (optional)

Shake well together (or beat the oil into the other ingredients using a wire whisk and a small bowl) and leave at
room temperature. Just before serving, stir in 1 to 2 tablespoons of minced green herbs such as parsley, tarragon,
basil or chives. Use any one or a combination of up to 3
herbs. Or you may omit the herbs altogether and still have a
basic French Dressing. When using mustard in the sauce it's
rather pointless to add fragile herbs.

Don't get carried away with too many of the various
optional ingredients. Choose from among them. Do experi-
ment with the amount of vinegar that satisfies your taste. I
prefer only ½ tablespoon of vinegar to 3 tablespoons of oil,
but the classic recipe calls for a ratio of 3 parts oil to 1 part
vinegar.

It doesn't matter too much whether your salad bowl is
glass, china or wood. But it should be large enough to get
both hands into it so that you can mix thoroughly. Turn the
greens gently at least six or seven times to be sure all the
leaves are coated. The taste of the dressing should be judged
on a salad leaf. Add dressing a little at a time and when each
leaf is glistening, stop! There should never be a well of dressing left in the bottom of the bowl after serving. This recipe
makes about enough for a medium head of Boston lettuce.
Quantities should not be made up in advance because the
oil loses its freshness quickly.

Some people add sliced cucumbers or avocado, among
other things, to a Green Salad. A Mixed Green Salad means
a mixture of various types of greens—not a mixture of various green things. Like tomatoes, mixed vegetables are a very

50

good salad in themselves but adulterating a green salad with them is one national sin I wish we could abolish.

TOMATO SALAD

serves 4

Red, ripe, juicy tomatoes are one of the very special joys of summer. Their rich, sweet taste should be savored with just the mildest of dressing, or, sometimes, just salt. Never choose pink, hard tomatoes encased in cellophane. Pick out your own very red, firm but ripe, tomatoes.

4 medium tomatoes
1 Tb chopped parsley
3 - 4 minced scallions (optional)
Sauce Vinaigrette

Slice the tomatoes from top to bottom with a sharp knife, using a light, sawing motion. This way of cutting them seems to hold the flesh and juices together better than cross-cutting. Cut out any green stem with the point of the knife. Arrange in overlapping slices and sprinkle with scallions and parsley. Drizzle Sauce Vinaigrette over all and serve at room temperature.

Note: Never refrigerate tomatoes. Their flavor evaporates in a matter of hours there. If you must have chilled tomatoes, cool them quickly by dropping them into a pot filled with ice cubes and cold water. If you are stuck with a few under-ripe tomatoes, let them ripen at room temperature but not in direct sunlight. Fairly ripe tomatoes will keep quite well at room temperature in a brown paper bag, for 4 or 5 days.

51

SPINACH AND MUSHROOM SALAD

serves 4

A pound looks like a lot of spinach, but a good many of the leaves must be discarded. Only small fresh, tender leaves should be used.

> *1 lb fresh young spinach*
> *½ lb fresh white mushrooms*
> *¼ cup French Dressing made with lemon juice*
> *freshly ground pepper*

Rinse the mushrooms with cold water, dry them in paper towels. Cut away the tough end of the stem, then slice through the cap and stem in ⅛-inch slices. The spinach may be prepared ahead of time as for any green salad but the mushrooms will darken if prepared in advance. Sprinkle the mushroom slices with a few drops of lemon juice and toss together with the spinach, French Dressing and pepper just before serving.

STRING BEAN SALAD

How I Learned to Stop Hating String Beans

My grandmother concocted this rather odd combination in an effort to teach me to like green beans without really noticing it. Her home-canned baby green beans may have had something to do with it too but top quality tiny whole green beans from a few luxury brands are just as good.

> *1 medium can tiny whole string beans*
> *8 - 10 cherry tomatoes, halved or ½ cup diced,*
> *ripe tomatoes*
> *4 medium scallions, sliced*
> *½ cup French Dressing*

Drain the string beans and mix gently with your hands with all other ingredients.

CAESAR SALAD

serves 10

This is the Crêpe Suzette of salads and should be tossed with great style and grace at the table. Accordingly, it must be served as a separate course, usually first.

1½ cups croutons
2 Tb garlic-flavored oil
1 clove garlic
½ cup olive oil
1 head of romaine
1 head of curly endive
salt
freshly ground black pepper

2 1-minute boiled eggs
Juice of a large lemon
8 to 10 anchovy fillets, chopped
½ cup freshly grated Parmesan or Romano cheese

Fry the croutons, either packaged or fresh ones made from stale French bread, in a little garlic-flavored oil until crisp. Drain on paper towels. Mash garlic and mix with ½ cup of oil. Tear salad greens into a large bowl. Add salt and freshly ground pepper to taste. Pour on oil and toss thoroughly. Pause eloquently, then break the eggs into the salad and with a sweeping gesture squeeze the lemon juice over it and toss madly again. Add chopped anchovies, croutons and cheese and toss very lightly.

53

salads

CUCUMBER SALAD

serves 4-6

The French cut out all the seeds, but if you choose young, small, dark green cucumbers, this should not be necessary. Europeans serve the cucumbers wilted while we usually go to great lengths to keep them crisp. I like them both ways but the wilted cucumbers absorb more dressing and have more flavor.

> *3 or 4 small dark-green cucumbers*
> *½ cup French Dressing*
> *salt and pepper*

Peel and slice the cucumbers thinly. Mix thoroughly with the French Dressing and season with salt and pepper. Store covered in a small, deep bowl in the refrigerator if you prefer the wilted version. Otherwise soak the peeled, but unsliced cucumbers in ice water for an hour and make the salad just prior to serving.

54

CUCUMBERS IN DILL

serves 4-6

This has vaguely Scandinavian overtones and is very complementary to boiled or broiled fish. It is also a cooling side dish to serve with highly spiced or curried foods.

> *3 medium cucumbers*
> *3 Tb chopped fresh dill weed*
> *¼ tsp salt*
> *1 cup commercial sour cream*

Peel and slice the cucumbers, sprinkle with dill and salt and place in a covered bowl in the refrigerator for at least ½ hour. Remove and drain off the water which the salt has extracted from the cucumbers. Arrange on a platter and cover with sour cream.

MIXED BUFFET SALAD

For a large number of people this is an excellent choice since it gets the hostess off the hook and allows each guest to indulge his own salad idiosyncrasies. This way, both the purists and the mad scientists of the salad bowl can be happy.

Arrange 3 or 4 bowls of different kinds of salad greens with diverse flavors and textures on the table. Surround them with smaller bowls of sliced raw mushrooms, diced cucumbers, canned artichoke hearts, toasted croutons, Greek olives, whole cherry tomatoes, crumbled blue cheese, palm hearts, diced avocado sprinkled with lemon juice, minced scallions, fresh chopped herbs, minced hard-cooked egg, and anything you especially fancy. You need not have all of these; three or four extra tidbits are enough. Just before serving time, mix each bowl of salad greens separately with a French Dressing and leave some extra dressing in a bowl or bottle on the table.

This is a good first-course salad because it leaves you free for last-minute kitchen duties while the guests are wandering among the salad choices.

55

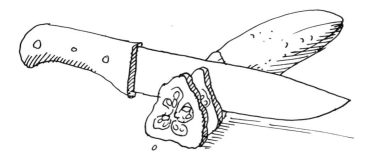

salads

SNACK SALADS

In my husband's birthplace, Strasbourg, eating is a regional pastime. Unlike other parts of France, there are *brasseries* and little *stubes* that serve between-meal tidbits at all hours of the day and night. After a creamy, rich wedge of Quiche Lorraine, a Strasbourgeois might pass the time with an order of wurst or cheese salad before he goes on to some Pâté en Croûte, more Zwicker (Alsatian white vin ordinaire) and perhaps a taste of the day's Tarte à l'Oignon. These cheese and sausage or cold cut salads don't fit into a menu really, but are lovely for midday or evening snacks in the summer.

> *Leftover roast beef, lamb, pork or veal*
> *Knockwurst, bologna, mortadella or soft salami*
> *Gruyère or Swiss cheese*
> *Sliced onions*
> *French Dressing*

Choose *one* of the above meats or cheeses and cut it into julienne strips. Add the thinly sliced onions. Pour on some Sauce Vinaigrette and toss with a fork. Marinate for about 1 hour in the refrigerator before serving with white wine or beer and hard rolls.

ZUCCHINI SALAD

serves 6-8

Young, raw zucchini has a slightly spicy flavor and a lovely texture. This salad is a bit like an uncooked ratatouille. It goes well with grilled steak, lamb chops or Italian sausages.

6 small, firm zucchini
  squashes
1 green Italian cooking
  pepper
3 small ripe tomatoes
3 scallions, sliced thinly

½ tsp salt
freshly ground black pepper
½ cup olive oil
1 to 2 Tb wine vinegar

Wash zucchini with a soft brush or cloth under cold running water to remove sand. Do not peel, but slice them thinly. Cut the green pepper in thin julienne strips. Spear the tomatoes, one at a time, on a long fork, then plunge them in boiling water for 10 seconds to loosen the skin. Peel and chop the tomatoes, taking care not to squeeze out too much juice. Put all ingredients in a bowl. Toss lightly, cover and serve about 1 hour later.

57

salads

COMPOSED SALADS

Composed salads made of vegetables, meat or fish and mayonnaise or other dressings are particularly compatible with hot weather and unexpected guests. There are several excellent brands of mayonnaise on the market but home-made mayonnaise is richer and fresher flavored. Once the technique is mastered, it really isn't too difficult or time-consuming. I use an electric mixer and finish with a wire whisk. This method is also good for Hollandaise and its derivative sauces.

Blender mayonnaise is absolutely painless to make and is somewhat lighter in texture since it will not absorb as much oil as a hand, or electric mixer-made, mayonnaise. Commercial brands are improved by beating some air and a few drops of lemon juice into them with a wire whisk.

MAYONNAISE

about 2 cups

These directions are for hand-beaten or electric-mixer mayonnaise. All ingredients and bowl should be at room temperature. Rinse the bowl in hot water and dry it to ensure that the egg yolks are warmed. Oil may be heated to tepid. Olive oil or plain unflavored vegetable oil may be used. The bowl must be glass or stainless steel, of about 3-quart capacity even though you are making only 2 cups of sauce.

3 egg yolks (U.S. Grade A "large")
1 Tb white wine vinegar or lemon juice
½ tsp salt
¼ tsp prepared or dry mustard
1½ cups olive or salad oil
2 Tb boiling water
additional salt, pepper, lemon juice or mustard to taste

Beat the egg yolks a couple of minutes until very thick and sticky. If using an electric mixer, beat on medium high speed and keep scraping egg yolks into the beater with a rubber spatula. Add the vinegar or lemon juice, salt and mustard and beat a few seconds longer. If using a wire whisk, prepare for prodigious and uninterrupted beating. You will have to figure out your own best way of keeping the bowl tilted, either between your knees or steadied in a larger pot with a dish towel stuffed under one side. One hand must beat and the other control the droplets of oil to be slowly incorporated into the yolks. Watch the oil constantly, not the sauce. Beating need not be too rapid but it must be constant.

Drop by drop, beat in about ½ cup of the oil. It should thicken to a heavy cream consistency before you rest. Then begin adding the oil in a thin stream or in 1-tablespoon additions, blending thoroughly after each one. If the sauce becomes too stiff, thin it out with a few drops of lemon juice or vinegar. Beat the 2 tablespoons of boiling water in to prevent curdling. Adjust seasoning. There! It's all over and should have taken about 10 minutes. If all you have is a curdled blob at some point in the preparation, you can bring it back this way:

59

SAVING THE MAYONNAISE

To a warm, dry bowl, add 1 teaspoon of prepared mustard and 1 tablespoon of the turned sauce. Beat with a mixer or wire whisk for a few minutes until the ingredients coagulate. Thoroughly incorporate the rest of the sauce, bit by bit.

salads

BLENDER MAYONNAISE

about 1¼ cups

As with hand-made sauce, ingredients should be at room temperature.

1 whole egg (U.S. Grade A "large")
¼ tsp dry mustard
½ tsp salt
1 Tb lemon juice or vinegar
1 cup olive or salad oil

Put the egg, mustard and salt into the blender, cover and blend at high speed for about 40 seconds. Turn off motor and add lemon juice or vinegar. Blend a few seconds. The next step can be a bit splattery so be sure you are well covered up. With the blender at high speed, pour the oil by droplets directly into the center of the whirling mixture. If the sauce thickens too quickly, add a few drops of lemon juice or vinegar. Taste for final seasonings. Blender mayonnaise will keep longer in the refrigerator than hand-made mayonnaise but it isn't advisable to keep either one more than a few days.

GREEN MAYONNAISE

about 2 cups

Delicious on fish and shellfish (an unexpected delight on a shrimp cocktail), this lovely green herbal sauce lifts even a few prosaic hard-cooked eggs into a thoroughly presentable main-course salad.

6 young spinach leaves	¼ cup watercress leaves
2 Tb chopped scallions	1 Tb fresh tarragon
⅓ cup parsley leaves	1½ cups mayonnaise

Blanch the spinach and scallions in a small amount of boiling water for 1 minute. Add remaining herbs and boil another minute. Drain, rinse with cold water and dry. Purée them in a mortar, or chop them fine and force through a sieve, or add them to blender mayonnaise before you run in the oil. Mix the puréed herbs into the 1½ cups of finished mayonnaise.

61

EGG SALAD ADVICE

1. Please leave off, cease and desist with the chopped celery. Instead, add chopped fresh tarragon, parsley and chives to the mayonnaise.
2. Throw in a few capers or leave out the tarragon and add some curry powder to the mayonnaise about ½ hour before combining it with the hard-cooked eggs.
3. Chop up some ripe olives and add them.
4. Garnish the salad with crossed anchovy fillets or a dollop of red or black caviar.
5. Serve it on a bed of crisp salad greens and decorate with chunks of drained tuna or some strips of ham or salami.

salads

SAUCE RÉMOULADE

about 2 cups

Another sauce that lost nearly everything in the translation to American restaurantese, this has come to mean anything from horseradish-flavored bottled chili sauce to even less definable orangy mixtures. Actually it is a salty, herbal mayonnaise used chiefly to garnish fish and shellfish.

> *1 tsp or more chopped capers*
> *1½ cups mayonnaise*
> *1 Tb each: minced chives, parsley and tarragon*
> *1 hard-cooked egg, minced*
> *3 or 4 mashed anchovy fillets, drained*

Wash the capers before you chop them if they are the large, salt-preserved type. Stir together all ingredients. Try this with any chilled, cooked shellfish.

SAUCE AÏOLI

about 1½ cups

Although this thick garlic mayonnaise is normally used as dressing for hot poached fish or boiled potatoes, it is also a welcome change from the ubiquitous Roquefort and onion dips so monotonously offered at summer parties. Serve Aïoli surrounded by a selection of fresh, raw summer vegetables cut into convenient pieces and this will obviate the salad course as well as the hors d'oeuvres. Aïoli can be approximated by pounding the garlic to a smooth paste and adding it to 1½ cups of store-bought mayonnaise, but it will not be quite as good.

1 crustless slice of day-old
  white bread
3 Tb wine vinegar
4 to 6 cloves garlic, roughly
  chopped
1 egg yolk

pinch of salt
1 to 1½ cups tepid olive oil
2 Tb lemon juice,
  approximately
3 Tb boiling water

Soak the bread in the vinegar about 10 minutes. Remove and squeeze dry. Put the garlic and bread into a mortar and pound with a pestle until it is a smooth paste. Beat in the egg yolk and salt. When the mixture is thick and sticky, start adding the oil by droplets and when about ⅓ of it is incorporated you may pour a little faster and use a wire whisk to complete the beating in. Add some lemon juice when the mixture becomes very heavy. Continue thinning with the boiling water as necessary. Aïoli should be about the consistency of commercial sour cream. If it curdles, the sauce may be reconstituted in the same manner as regular mayonnaise (see recipe).

GREEN GODDESS SALAD

serves 6

Considered a "classic" of California cuisine, this luncheon salad was created in honor of George Arliss, who was appearing in a play called "The Green Goddess" in 1915 in San Francisco. Since it almost qualifies as a regional dish, there are numerous versions and you can work out your own and add another theory to the din.

¼ cup minced parsley
2 Tb fresh tarragon, minced
¼ cup chives, minced
6 - 8 anchovy fillets
2 cups mayonnaise

¾ cup French Dressing
  with garlic
1 large head romaine
1½ lbs cooked scallops,
  lobster, shrimp or
  crabmeat (or a mixture)

Mix together the parsley, tarragon, chives and anchovies. Beat them into the mayonnaise with a fork along with about ¼ cup of the French Dressing. (Don't use an electric mixer because all the herbs will cling to the beaters.) Tear the romaine into rather large pieces and toss with the remaining French Dressing. Arrange the salad greens on six individual chilled plates. Working quickly, mix the cooked seafood with the green mayonnaise and pile lightly onto the romaine. Garnish with additional minced parsley. You may also simply heap the seafood onto the salad greens and spoon the dressing over the top.

TONGUE AND CHICKEN SALAD

serves 6

I have eaten everything from pineapple to walnuts in chicken salads but rarely anything as complementary as tongue. The temptation to make a sandwich and forget the salad must be resisted because the salad is unforgettable.

12 large slices of cooked tongue (⅛-inch thick)	2 Tb minced parsley
	1 small white onion
2 cups cooked, cubed chicken	1 cup mayonnaise
	¼ tsp dry mustard
1 Tb minced celery	watercress
3 hard-cooked eggs	

Cut the tongue into julienne strips about 1½ inches long. Add it to the cubed chicken, celery and parsley. Grate the onion into the mayonnaise; blend in the mustard. Fold into the meat mixture. Serve each portion on a bed of watercress and garnish with half a hard-cooked egg.

Variation: Add a pair of calf's sweetbreads, prepared in the following manner and cut into small pieces.

65

BASIC PREPARATION OF SWEETBREADS

Buy very fresh sweetbreads and use them the same day. Plunge them in ice water for 1 hour. Remove and place in a small pan with cold water to cover. Add a small onion stuck with 2 cloves, a piece of bay leaf, ¼ tsp salt and the juice of ½ lemon. Bring them slowly to the boil and simmer them for about 15 minutes. Plunge again into ice water for 5 minutes, then remove tubes and membranes. This procedure must be followed prior to using any recipe involving sweetbreads.

FRENCH POTATO SALAD

about 6 cups

This is a classic French version of the salad so dear to the heart of every Southerner. Dixie style, it is usually filled with eggs, olives, pimentoes, pickles, onions and lavishly bound with a rich mayonnaise. Although I remember it fondly, I have grown to prefer this more subtly flavored French-style potato salad. It may be an accompaniment to wafer-thin slices of Smithfield ham, hot or cold fried chicken, charcoal grilled meats or, elaborately garnished in the Alsatian style, may serve as the main course.

8 to 10 medium all-purpose potatoes (do not use Idaho or russets as they crumble when sliced)	2 Tb wine vinegar
	½ tsp salt
	1 tsp dry mustard
	7 Tb olive oil
4 to 5 Tb dry white wine	6 scallions, minced
½ cup fresh parsley, minced	

Scrub the potatoes and boil them in their jackets in salted water until just tender when pierced with a very sharp kitchen fork. Drain and shake over low heat to dry thoroughly. Peel them as hot as you can handle them. The potatoes should still be warm when the dressing is added. Slice them in ⅛-inch rounds and place in a large mixing bowl. As you put in each layer of potatoes, sprinkle with some of the wine. Next beat the vinegar, salt and mustard powder together in a small bowl with a wire whisk, or electric mixer. Beat in the oil slowly until you have a creamy emulsion. Taste for salt and pepper. Then taste the potatoes for saltiness before adding any more to the dressing. Sprinkle the potatoes with the minced scallions and parsley. Pour on the dressing and mix lightly with your hands taking care not to break the potatoes any more than necessary. If the salad is not to be served at once, cover it with plastic wrap and leave it at room temperature, then turn out into a lettuce-lined platter and garnish with all or any of the following: Sliced hard-cooked eggs, skinless and boneless sardines, anchovy fillets, half-circles of hard salami, kosher dill gherkins, radish roses, ripe or green olives, drained tuna fish or smoked eel.

This gloriously decorated platter takes a while to make but it is well worth the effort. Naturally, if the potato salad is to be served as a side dish, eggs and pickles are quite enough garnish, and are all the classic French recipe calls for.

DIXIE STYLE POTATO SALAD

There may not be as many disagreements about what goes into this rococo production as there are about Brunswick Stew, but I doubt it. This one was served on witheringly hot summer Sundays with enormous platters of fried chicken, pitchers of iced tea, and hot biscuits straight from the inferno of the kitchen. The whole heavy, rich, splendid midday gluttony ended with dishes of soft peach ice cream cranked to smoothness under the shade of a chinaberry tree.

10 medium-large all-purpose "boiling" potatoes
1 cup chopped scallions
3 hard-cooked eggs, chopped
1 green pepper, chopped fine
½ cup sweet pickles, chopped coarsely
¼ cup celery, minced
2 Tb chopped, pimento-stuffed olives
¼ cup minced parsley
1 to 1½ cups mayonnaise

Boil the potatoes in their jackets in salted water until just tender, about 30 minutes. Peel and slice or dice them. Blend in all ingredients and enough mayonnaise to bind the salad together. Use a wooden fork and spoon, lifting and folding the potatoes as gently as possible. Taste for seasoning and add salt or pepper if required. Turn into a large shallow bowl or platter and decorate with the garnishes listed below. *Garnish:* Sliced hard-cooked eggs, dill or sweet gherkins, strips of canned pimento, sliced cucumbers, stuffed green olives or (my preference) black Italian olives.

salads

KIDNEY BEAN SALAD

serves 4

I think this mish-mosh of flavors is Pennsylvania Dutch in origin. It is my analysis of what I ate many times in western Pennsylvania with a few alterations I prefer to the more authentic sweet-sour version. It sounds ghastly but even those who cast a wary eye on it end up fighting over the last bean. Since the ingredients are usually on hand it is a lifesaver when drop-in guests stay for lunch or dinner.

2 cups canned red kidney beans
½ cup minced scallions or red Italian onion
2 Tb chopped kosher dill pickles (in Pennsylvania, limp
*   sweet pickles)*
1 hard-cooked egg, chopped
¾ cup mayonnaise (in Pennsylvania, boiled salad dressing)

Drain the kidney beans and rinse lightly under cold running water. Drain thoroughly. Combine all ingredients and mix gently. Chill for at least 1 hour. This is good served with a variety of sliced cold sausages and beer.

ANOTHER KIDNEY BEAN SALAD
serves 4

The combination of ingredients is somewhat less alarming in this version and may be adapted to almost any kind of cooked dried beans. One might substitute pinto, marrow, soldier beans or lentils.

2 cups cooked or canned red kidney beans	¼ tsp dry mustard
	⅛ tsp curry powder (or less)
1 Bermuda or red Italian onion	1 Tb vinegar
	1 Tb olive oil
¼ tsp salt	1 clove garlic, minced

Drain the beans thoroughly and place in a small, deep bowl. Halve the onion and slice it very thin. Add it to the beans. Mix the salt, mustard and curry powder with the vinegar, then add the oil and garlic. Stir briskly and pour over the beans. Mix gently with your hands and do not mash the beans. Cover tightly and store overnight or at least 12 hours at room temperature. The various flavors will not ripen properly in the refrigerator.

CRABMEAT SALAD

"Fresh" crabmeat, all picked out, is actually frozen down in Louisiana somewhere and sealed in cans which are opened and thawed out by retail fish dealers. Backfin is cheaper than chunk crabmeat, just as tasty, but not as attractive. Frozen crabmeat is quite delicious. I just object to being told constantly that it is "fresh." Processed pasteurized canned crabmeat is not worth discussing; have chicken salad instead. Allow about ¼ lb of crabmeat per person. Pick over the crabmeat carefully with your fingers so that you can feel the little bits of shell or fin that are always there. Heap it on individual romaine beds, ladle on some Sauce Rémoulade and garnish with lemon slices.

salads

LOBSTER SALAD

serves 6

Always buy live lobsters and cook them yourself. Most precooked lobsters are dried out and of dubious freshness. I saw one fish dealer actually wash the cooked meat under running water. He got rid of the roe, the tomalley (green liver) and the flavor in one fell swoop. Never wash seafood after it is cooked.

Various humane ways of cooking live lobster have been proposed. But since there are no living witnesses to vouch for any of them, I suppose this is as good a method as any. Prepare the following Court Bouillon, simmer it for 20 minutes, then plunge the live lobster into it.

> *1 pint dry white wine*
> *4 quarts boiling water*
> *2 Tb salt*
> *bay leaf, thyme, crushed red pepper*
> *1 peeled onion stuck with 2 cloves*

If you cook shellfish or fish often, you can strain this broth and save for use another time. Lobster should be cooked 5 minutes for the first pound and 3 minutes for each additional pound.

Lay the lobster on its back. Clip open the tail shell with heavy kitchen shears. Cut through the body with a large heavy knife. If the lobster is large you may need a cleaver for the body. (Incidentally, 3-pounders are a good buy for salads as they are cheaper and just as juicy if you don't overcook them.) Remove the sac near the head. Reserve the roe or coral, and eat the green tomalley (cook's dividend) on a piece of toast.

Pick out the meat from the body cavity, especially the joints where the small legs are connected. Remove the claw meat and tail meat in one piece if possible. Slice the tail meat into rounds. Chill the claw, tail and body meat in airtight plastic bags, separately.

Rub the red coral through a sieve and beat it into a good mayonnaise. Arrange some of each kind of lobster meat on a bed of chilled greens on each plate. Put a spoonful of sauce in the center. Garnish with hard-cooked eggs, a sprinkle of chopped mixed green herbs (parsley, chives and chervil) and pass additional sauce at the table. One 3-pound lobster will yield enough meat for salad for six persons. If serving individual lobsters, allow a 1- to 1½-pound lobster per person.

TUNA SALAD

serves 2

It seems absurd to include a recipe for this popular dish we all tasted along with our first peanut butter sandwiches. However, because tuna is so much used and so dreadfully abused, I insist upon offering my version of this American favorite. It is a quickie and serves 2 as a main course.

1 can white, solid-pack tuna fish	*2 hard-cooked eggs, shelled and chopped*
3 scallions with some green, minced	*½ cup mayonnaise*
	romaine
1 Tb capers, drained	*Italian oil-cured black olives*

Drain the tuna and break it into small chunks with a fork. Mix it with the scallions and capers, then carefully fold in the hard-cooked eggs and mayonnaise. Pile lightly on washed and dried romaine leaves and garnish generously with the black olives. Of course you can always make sandwiches with it too, but use freshly toasted bread and serve right away.

CANNELLINI WITH TUNA

serves 6

Cannellini are white kidney beans. I first ate them in Rome served cold with oil and lemon. I made my version of this dish for some Roman friends who gave it their seal of approval. Italian foods distributors have made cannellini available in most supermarkets.

1 medium can cannellini	*¼ cup olive oil*
(about 1½ cups)	*salt and pepper*
1 can white chunk-style tuna	*1 lemon*
2 scallions, minced	*1 Tb parsley, chopped*

Drain and rinse the beans under cold water. Drain well. Combine beans with the minced scallions and olive oil. Arrange individual portions on small plates, sprinkle with salt, pepper and parsley. Garnish with drained chunks of tuna and lemon wedges. This is best served as a first course at an otherwise light luncheon or supper.

72

CRACKED CRAB

Fresh crabs are almost totally unavailable unless you catch them yourself. If you manage to get some live ones, boil them in salted water seasoned with chilis, bay leaf, onion and cumin seed until they turn bright red. Cooking time varies with the size of the crabs, but even the largest Atlantic blue crab should not take more than 10 minutes. For local varieties, ask the fish dealer's wife's advice. Picking out the meat is laborious and a terrible waste too. Just crack the claws, pull off the back and remove the spongy substance under it, then replace the back shell. Turn the crab on its back and pull off the underside shell. Provide little forks and picks and let each guest fend for himself. Pass a bowl of mayonnaise or Sauce Rémoulade.

Fish and Shellfish

Traditionally fish was served as a third or even a fourth course at formal dinners. But since that sumptuous era of dining has long since disappeared there seems no reason why fish is served so seldom as a main course. A whole, stuffed baked fish is simple to prepare and makes a dramatic presentation. Served hot or cold, the delicacy and lightness of fish should be enjoyed especially during the summer months.

There are endless ways to deal with the great variety of fish from American waters. Fish are divided into either the "fat" or "lean" class. Any fish may be substituted for another in the same class for almost any recipe. Shellfish are all lean. Any good fish dealer will be able to tell you which class the fish you select falls into. When buying whole fish, allow ½ pound per person.

Buying Fish

Fresh fish should not smell "fishy." Its eyes should be bright and bulgy—not flat and opaque. Gills should be bright red, the skin glistening and the flesh firm to the touch. Filleted fish should be almost odorless or, at most, smell faintly of sea water. Frozen fish *should* be odorless if it is indeed hurtled from the boat to the freezer as is generally claimed. But it isn't. Probably the lack of freshness is the fault of the grocer rather than the processor, since frozen fish does not keep well indefinitely. Except for cod and haddock to use in chowders, I have not found any satisfactory frozen fish.

Cooking Fish

Whether you are poaching, broiling, baking or frying fish, you should keep in mind that it cooks very quickly. There is no remedy for overdone fish; it simply falls to bits when it is served. Handle the fish as little as possible while you are cooking it to avoid breaking it. It is difficult to give precise times for cooking fish because the size of the fish and the amount of heat vary. Frequent testing with a fork or a toothpick, until the fish is easily pierced, will determine when it is done. As a further precaution, make a small incision with a small knife in the thickest part of the fish to be certain it is cooked through.

Fish Sauces

Saucing adds variety to the bland flavor of many fish. The base of nearly all fish sauces is Court Bouillon, which is then reduced, enriched and thickened with egg yolks, cream and butter.

COURT BOUILLON

2 cups dry white wine
1 quart water
fish trimmings (heads and
    bones)
1 medium onion stuck with
2 cloves

½ large bay leaf
1 tsp salt
6 whole peppercorns
3 - 4 sprigs of parsley
sprig of fresh thyme or pinch
    of dried thyme

Put all ingredients in a soup kettle and bring to the boil. Simmer for at least 20 minutes with the lid askew. Strain, then proceed with your recipe.

fish and shellfish

SAUCE PARISIENNE

2 cups

This is a simple sauce that takes only about 10 minutes to make but it will lift even a plain poached flounder fillet into the realm of la grande cuisine.

2 Tb butter
2½ Tb flour
1½ cups boiling,
    concentrated Court
    Bouillon

2 egg yolks
½ cup heavy cream
salt and pepper
lemon juice

Melt the butter in a heavy-bottomed saucepan and stir in the flour. Cook on low heat, stirring constantly, for two minutes. Do not let the mixture brown. You now have a white roux. Pour in the Court Bouillon all at once and stir vigorously with a wire whisk. Continue stirring and boiling over high heat for about 2 minutes. Set aside. Beat the egg yolks and stir in the heavy cream. Add a little of the hot sauce to the egg and cream mixture, beating with a wooden spoon. Gradually beat in the rest of the sauce, then return it to the saucepan. Add salt and pepper and a few drops of lemon juice. You may add more cream if you prefer the sauce thinner and more butter if you wish a richer sauce.

DERIVATIVE SAUCES

SAUCE MORNAY. Add grated Gruyère or Swiss cheese, about 4 tablespoons.

SAUCE AURORE. Add 2 tablespoons of tomato paste and 2 tablespoons of mixed basil and parsley, minced.

TARRAGON SAUCE. Combine 1 cup of white wine with 4 tablespoons of fresh, minced tarragon and reduce the mixture to 3 tablespoons over high heat. Add it to the Sauce Parisienne along with 1 tablespoon of butter and 2 tablespoons of chopped parsley.

MUSTARD SAUCE. Add 2 tablespoons of very strong prepared mustard and 3 or 4 tablespoons of butter to the basic sauce.

CAPER SAUCE. Add 3 tablespoons of drained capers and beat in 2 or 3 tablespoons of softened sweet butter.

Note: Sauces that are heavily butter-enriched tend to separate if left standing. If not to be used immediately, the sauce should be covered with a thin film of cream. Reheat over medium heat, beating rapidly with a wire whisk or wooden spoon. Although these are rich sauces, they should *seem* light; their flavoring should be subtle and the texture velvety.

POACHED WHOLE FISH

Almost any whole fish is suitable for gentle simmering in an aromatic Court Bouillon. Poached fish is generally served with one of the preceding fish sauces, but the flavor of a fine, fresh fish doesn't actually *require* anything more elaborate than melted butter, parsley and lemon. Allow ½ pound per person.

Wash the fish under cold running water and wrap it in a double thickness of cheesecloth with long ends if you do not have a special fish kettle. A fish kettle has its own rack and is useful for steaming shellfish and cooking corn among other things. Using the ends of the cloth as handles, lower the fish into the simmering Court Bouillon, letting the ends hang out over the edges of the pan. It should be long enough and deep enough to hold the fish plus an inch of liquid. Simmer the fish 8 to 10 minutes per pound. Test for doneness by inserting a toothpick near the backbone. Remove the fish and drain it on a dish towel.

A whole large fish is easier to serve at the table if the body has first been skinned; but leave the head and tail intact. Peel the skin off one side with your fingers, then roll the fish gently over onto a heated platter and skin the other side. Often the skin will cling to the dish towel, removing the skin for you. Pour butter or sauce over the whole fish and warm it or brown it lightly under the broiler before serving. Pass extra sauce in a pitcher or sauceboat at the table.

POACHED FISH FILLETS

When buying fillets, be sure to ask the fish dealer for some trimmings. Otherwise your Court Bouillon will be insipid. Very thin fillets, such as flounder, are easier to handle if they are first rolled up and tied with soft white string. The fish will hold its cylindrical shape after cooking even though you must remove the string before serving.

Fillets of flounder, fluke, lemon or gray sole will be cooked in about 5 minutes if arranged flat; they will cook in from 8 to 12 minutes if rolled up. The Court Bouillon must be maintained just under the boiling point or you will have a pan of fish flakes for your trouble. When the fish tests tender with a toothpick or fork, remove it to a cloth dish towel, then roll it gently onto a heated flameproof platter. Fillets should be sauced, or buttered, then run under the broiler for a quick heating up.

POACHED FRESH SALMON

Salmon is nearly always cut into steaks and it is invariably expensive but there is very little waste. A whole poached salmon of about 8 pounds makes a magnificent buffet centerpiece. The service of this needs a practiced hand.

Have the salmon steaks cut about 1-inch thick. Allow 1 per person. Ask for some extra trimmings. Make the Court Bouillon (see recipe), and simmer the salmon steaks for about 10 minutes. Start testing after 7 minutes to be certain you don't overcook them. Salmon, like swordfish, is a fat fish, but its large flakes easily become dry and unpalatable. Many people broil salmon and swordfish steaks but I think the method is entirely too drying.

When they are done, drain the steaks on a dish towel, then transfer to a platter and serve hot or chilled with Hollandaise Sauce. A mayonnaise to which you have added a few tablespoons of finely diced, seeded cucumber and some chopped tarragon, is a particularly appropriate summmer sauce for cold fish.

fish and shellfish

HUSH PUPPIES

serves 6

Why this deep-fried fritter received its inscrutable name has several explanations. One I cling to is that fishermen sitting around their campfire frying the day's catch tossed these fish-flavored bits to their dogs with the admonition, "Hush, puppy." They are nearly always served at Southern fish fries cooked in the fat the fish were fried in. But they can be fried in plain salad oil too.

1 cup cornmeal	¾ cup milk
¾ tsp salt	1 egg, beaten
¼ tsp pepper	2 Tb bacon fat or melted
2 tsp baking powder	butter
1 medium onion, minced	

Mix the dry ingredients together, then blend in the milk, egg, fat and onion. Do not overmix. Drop by rounded teaspoons into deep hot fat and fry until golden, 3 to 5 minutes. Drain on absorbent paper and serve very hot.

STRIPED BASS BÉARNAISE

serves 4

Have the fish cleaned but left whole. You may have the head removed if you just can't bear the reproach in its eyes, but it won't look as good.

1 3-pound striped bass
1 qt Court Bouillon (see recipe)
1 cup Sauce Béarnaise (see recipe)

Poach the bass in the Court Bouillon about 30 minutes. Remove to a towel, peel off the skin between the head and tail, then gently roll the fish over onto a preheated platter. Peel the skin off the other side. Pour the Sauce Béarnaise over the fish and garnish the platter with little cherry tomatoes. Serve with boiled new potatoes.

TROUT IN BROWN BUTTER

serves 4

If you are lucky enough to have a source of fresh trout or live near a hatchery, this is a splendid recipe. All the frozen trout I have ever tried have been disasters and I wouldn't recommend substituting them.

> *4 small fresh-water trout*
> *1 qt boiling Court Bouillon (see recipe)*
> *¼ lb sweet butter*
> *lemon wedges*

Lay the trout in a shallow pan and cover with the boiling Court Bouillon. Hold at the simmer point 10 to 15 minutes, depending on the size of the trout. When they are tender but still firm, drain them on a dish towel and remove to a hot platter. Heat the butter in a small heavy saucepan until it turns a rich, light brown. Pour over the trout and garnish with lemon wedges. Plain boiled potatoes are the only thing to serve with this purist's delight. *81*

fish and shellfish

FILLETS OF SOLE MARGUERY

serves 4

Named for the famous chef and owner of the Restaurant Marguery in Paris, this dish is an elegant classic. Wine, butter, cream and eggs are blended into a buttery sauce glazing a platter of poached sole, oysters and shrimp. In our summer version, mussels will have to take the place of oysters.

8 *small fillets of gray or*	*juice of 1 lemon*
lemon sole or flounder	*1 cup thick white sauce*
16 medium-size shrimp	*(Béchamel)*
16 medium-size mussels	*2 egg yolks*
2 Tb melted butter	*4 Tb butter*
¾ cup dry white wine	*salt*

¼ cup parsley, minced

Make the white sauce (see recipe). Preheat oven to 400° F. Butter a large rectangular pan and lay the fish fillets in it. Salt the fish lightly and pour the wine and lemon juice around the fish. Spoon a bit of melted butter onto each fillet. Bake for 15 minutes, basting once. While the fillets are baking, poach the shrimp, shell and devein them. Open the mussels by boiling in water and set aside to keep warm. Carefully lift out the fillets and arrange them on a hot, heatproof platter. Reserve pan juices. Decorate with the shelled shrimp and mussels. Over high heat reduce the pan juices to ¾ cup. Beat the egg yolks into the white sauce, then add the fish liquid, stirring with a whisk. Beat in butter and pour the sauce over the fish platter. Glaze under the broiler. Sprinkle with parsley and serve.

BAKED FISH FILLETS

serves 4

When in doubt, this is a safe method of preparation for any fish fillet. Even though you do have to use the oven, fillets bake in a few minutes and are easy for a quick dinner. Choose any of the flounder species; or fillets of bluefish, shad, perch, bass or red snapper are some other suggestions. Allow 1 large or 2 small fillets per person.

>*4 large fish fillets*
>*½ cup dry white wine*
>*4 Tb butter*
>*salt and pepper, or rose paprika*
>*minced parsley*

Preheat the oven to 400° F. Lay the fillets in a buttered oblong pan just large enough to hold them. Reduce the white wine over high heat to ¼ cup. Add the butter to the wine and when it is melted, spoon a little of the mixture over each fillet. Sprinkle lightly with salt and pepper or a bit of hot Hungarian rose paprika. Bake 15 minutes, basting frequently with the remaining wine and butter and pan juices. Test for doneness and remove to a heated platter. Sprinkle with parsley and pour on a bit more melted butter. Serve at once with plain boiled new potatoes, a green salad and some chilled, dry white wine.

83

fish and shellfish

RED SNAPPER ISLE DES SAINTES

serves 4

I have no idea if snappers even exist in the Caribbean waters surrounding this tiny Breton fishermen's community off the coast of Guadeloupe. In this remote place with no hotels, plumbing or restaurants "Madame in the blue house" cooks superbly on a charcoal burner for the occasional yachtsmen who come ashore. Snapper serves well to reproduce Madame's peppery fish.

> *1 3-pound red snapper*
> *¼ lb butter*
> *juice of 1 lemon*
> *3 tiny red-hot fresh chili peppers, minced*
> *lemon slices*

Have the snapper cleaned, boned and split. Ideally, the snapper should be charcoal broiled, but if this is impossible, remove the broiling rack and turn the broiler to its highest setting. Oil the rack thoroughly. Dry the fish on paper towels and grease both sides liberally with melted butter. Lay the fish, flesh side down, on a double thickness of aluminum foil. Mix the peppers with the butter and lemon juice. Spoon a little of the mixture over the fish. Broil, skin side up, 3 inches from the heat for about 5 minutes. When the skin is nicely browned, roll the fish over onto the oiled rack and discard the foil. Spoon the peppery butter over the flesh side. Broil 5 minutes longer, basting once or twice. Begin testing and when the fish is done transfer it to a hot platter. Heat the remaining butter and lemon juice to foaming and pour it over the fish. Garnish with thin rounds of lemon. Serve with an inexpensive, icy cold, dry white wine. This is *only* for guests known to possess courage and a love of hot food.

SMALL WHOLE BROILED FISH

Flounder and porgie, fresh mackerel, brook trout, fresh sardines, mullet, perch, lemon sole, sunfish and weakfish are all good choices when they weigh less than 1½ pounds. Or get the very freshest local fish you can buy and have it gutted but left whole. Allow one whole fish per person. Wash and dry them, then rub them inside and out with the cut side of half a lemon. Salt them inside and out and massage well with softened butter.

Do NOT preheat the broiler since you will want to turn the fish to brown on both sides and preheating would overcook it. The fish should be laid directly on a well-oiled broiler rack and not on aluminum foil. The juices would collect in the foil and spoil the lovely brown crustiness of the skin.

Broil the fish on medium heat about 3 inches from the flame for about 5 minutes. Brush the fish with melted butter and turn carefully, using two spatulas to roll the fish gently over. Brush the uncooked side with melted butter and broil for another 5 minutes. Test for doneness with a toothpick; broiling time will vary enormously depending on whether you are cooking a flat flounder or a plump trout. Thus a long, thin fish weighing 1½ pounds will cook much more quickly than a short, thick one weighing less. Serve with Brown Butter (See Trout in Brown Butter) poured over the fish and garnish with thin lemon wedges.

COLD TROUT WITH GREEN MAYONNAISE

serves 4

On a really hot day, nothing could be more pleasant for lunch or dinner than this delicate dish. Allow one small trout for each person. Poach it in Court Bouillon 10 to 15 minutes. Drain and chill the fish, well covered with plastic wrap. Before serving, peel the fish, garnish each plate with sliced hard-cooked eggs and a few sprigs of parsley. Serve with a bowl of Green Mayonnaise (see recipe). Striped bass may also be prepared in this way, but, since small striped bass are illegal, serve 1 fish for 2 or 3 people.

> *4 small fresh-water trout*
> *1 qt boiling Court Bouillon*
> *4 eggs, hard-boiled*
> *parsley*
> *Green Mayonnaise*

SEA SQUAB PROVENCAL

serves 4

Sea squab is the euphemism created by sensitive fish dealers for the lowly blowfish. Possibly the least expensive fish on the Northeast coast and probably the ugliest, it is nevertheless delicious. It is always sold cleaned, skinned and beheaded so that it resembles a very large shrimp with a backbone. Overcooking these morsels turns them into little rubber balls. I use certain elements typical of southern French cooking, thus the name for my purely Long Island invention.

1½ lbs blowfish
⅓ cup olive oil
2 cloves garlic, minced
1 onion, chopped
½ bay leaf
sprig of fresh thyme or
pinch of dried thyme

1 lb ripe red tomatoes
  or 1 can whole Italian
  plum tomatoes
½ cup dry white wine
parsley
salt and pepper
flour

Salt and pepper the blowfish and dust them lightly with flour. Sauté them in the olive oil in a heavy skillet until golden. Remove fish and set aside while you make the sauce. Peel and chop the fresh tomatoes in a bowl so as not to lose the juice. In the same skillet, cook the onions until soft along with the garlic, adding a bit of olive oil if necessary. Add the tomatoes, white wine and herbs and simmer uncovered for 30 minutes. (Recipe may be prepared in advance up to this point.) Return the blowfish to the skillet and let them simmer in the sauce for 5 minutes to heat them through. Serve sprinkled with parsley. Rice is good with this.

fish and shellfish

BAKED STRIPED BASS
WITH POTATOES

serves 8

Although the preparation involves a good deal of slicing and chopping, when you are finished you have a complete meal and needn't fuss with side dishes. All the flavors enhance each other but each remains distinct.

olive oil
1 striped bass, weighing
    about 6 lbs
juice of 2 lemons
salt and pepper
3 large onions, sliced thin

1 cup chopped parsley
2 green peppers, seeded
    and sliced thin
6 medium "boiling"
    potatoes, peeled and
    sliced paper thin

3 ripe tomatoes, sliced thin

Oil a shallow pyrex or earthenware dish large enough to hold the fish. The fish should be cleaned with the backbone removed, but not split. The head may be cut off if you prefer. Wash the fish, dry it and rub inside and out with lemon juice and salt. Lay about ⅓ of the onions and 3 tablespoons of parsley in the fish's cavity. Sauté the remaining onions and sliced green peppers until softened. Arrange potato slices on the bottom of the baking dish. Sprinkle with salt and pepper. Lay the fish on top of the potatoes and cover all with the sautéed onions and green peppers. Drizzle olive oil over the fish and vegetables. Cover with a double thickness of foil and bake 40 minutes in a 400° F. oven. Uncover, baste with pan juices and arrange the sliced tomatoes over the top. Drizzle with oil and continue baking, uncovered, for another 20 minutes. Sprinkle with remaining parsley and serve in the baking dish. A good Aïoli (see recipe) is a "must" with this fish.

BROILED SHAD

serves 4

Though commonly thought to be a spring fish, shad is an Atlantic deep-sea fish available most of the year. When the rivers warm in spring, the shad swim in from the sea to spawn, and it is then that the greatly prized shad roe is in season. The fish itself is also a great delicacy. Buck shad is quite cheap. But because the shad contains an aggravating number of fine bones, it must be filleted and it takes a real master to do it. This doubles the price.

1 3-pound shad, boned and cut into serving pieces
½ cup melted butter
salt and pepper
capers
lemon slices

Oil and preheat the broiler. Lay the shad pieces on the broiler rack and brush with melted butter. Sprinkle with salt and pepper. Broil about three inches from the heat for about 8 minutes. Baste frequently with the melted butter and resign yourself to watching the fish during almost the entire broiling time to be certain that it does not dry out or overcook. Shad is a fat fish and broils well. Do not turn the fish. The preheated broiler will cook the underside, although it won't brown it. When the fish tests done with a toothpick, lift it onto a heated platter or, preferably, the heated dinner plates. The less handling any fish receives, the more likely it will be to reach the table in an attractive, unbroken condition. Pour a little melted butter on each portion, scatter with a few capers and garnish with lemon slices. Bluefish is excellent prepared in this way. Thin fillets, such as flounder, are not suitable for broiling. Ratatouillle, a marvelous mélange of fresh vegetables, goes well with broiled fish.

DEEP-FRIED FRESH SARDINES

serves 3-4

Deep frying is without a doubt the dreariest way in the world to cook fish except for these little summer delights (or smelts in winter). Children and people with underdeveloped palates enjoy small thick fish fillets done this way and the method is well within the capability of any fourth grader.

Allow 3 or 4 sardines per person, depending on how large the fish are. An expert fish dealer will know how to gut these tiny fish without splitting them open. They are always fried whole.

12 fresh sardines	*dry breadcrumbs*
flour	*salt and pepper*
2 eggs beaten with 1 tsp	*1 qt plain salad oil*
water	*lemon slices*

Wash the sardines under cold running water. Squeeze them gently and run your finger inside to be certain they are quite clean. Dry them thoroughly and dust with flour. Dip them in the beaten egg, then in breadcrumbs mixed with salt and pepper. Press the crumbs into the fish between your palms so that the crumbs will adhere. Lay them on a rack to dry as you finish the breading. In a deep heavy saucepan or electric fryer, heat the salad oil hot enough to brown a day-old cube of bread in 30 seconds. You should be able to fry 3 or 4 fish at a time. They will cook in 3 to 5 minutes. If you have to turn them over, roll them with a wooden spoon and don't pierce the crust because it will make the fat spit and the fish crust soggy. Remove each batch and drain on paper towels. Keep them warm in a low oven until all are fried. Serve them stacked crisscross on a hot platter surrounded by lemon slices.

SCALLOPED SCALLOPS, SHRIMP AND FLOUNDER

serves 12

This is a dish I devised to cope with those evenings when I don't quite know how many guests are coming, or when. It can be made in the morning and reheated at serving time. Since the dish requires no knife and the casserole keeps it warm, this is practical for a buffet.

> 1½ lbs scallops
> Court Bouillon (see recipe)
> 2 lbs small shrimp
> 12 flounder fillets
> 1 lb mushrooms, sliced
> 3 Tb butter
> 4 cups Sauce Parisienne (see recipe)
> 2 Tb chopped parsley or tarragon, or both

Cut the scallops across the grain into bite-size pieces. Put them in a strainer, wire basket or a cheesecloth bag and cook them in the barely bubbling Court Bouillon for 1 minute. Remove and drain. Wash the shrimp and cook them for 2 minutes in the same Court Bouillon. Shell and devein them. Roll up the flounder fillets and fasten them with a toothpick. Put them in the Court Bouillon for about 5 minutes. Drain them and save the fish stock to make your Sauce Parisienne. Sauté the mushrooms for a few minutes in the butter until they are rather dry. Make the Sauce Parisienne and add the mushrooms. Butter an ovenproof casserole and stand the rolled fish fillets inside its perimeter. Fill the center with the scallops and shrimp.* Pour the Sauce Parisienne over all. Bake in a 450° F. oven about 5 minutes or until hot through. Strew with the chopped herbs and serve.
*Note: Recipe may be made in advance up to this point. The Sauce Parisienne will have to be gently reheated and beaten with a wire whisk before baking.

fish and shellfish

AMAGANSETT BOUILLABAISSE

serves 12-14

My bouillabaisse has little in common with the famous soup of Marseille which is always full of eel and never contains lobster. You may put fresh eel in along with any firm-fleshed fishes, preferably of varying sizes and textures. I loathe boiled eel so I have omitted that and added all the fish and shellfish I do like. This is a splendid summer Sunday brunch dish and I always serve it outside where the lawn can serve as a napkin and wastebasket for all the shells.

2 live lobsters, 1½ lbs each
2 3-lb sea bass or stripers
1 lb shrimp
3 lbs porgie or fresh
   mackerel (or both, mixed)
1 qt mussels
2 qts cherrystone clams
   or 2 qts steamers
olive oil
3 medium onions, sliced
3 large cloves garlic,
   minced
1½ qts dry white wine
(Almaden Chablis is a
   good inexpensive choice)

3 qts water, lightly salted
large can Italian peeled
   tomatoes or 1½ lbs fresh
   peeled, chopped tomatoes
1 Tb monosodium
   glutamate
1 bay leaf, 2 sprigs thyme,
   10 peppercorns, tied in
   a cheesecloth bag
several loaves of French
   bread
½ tsp saffron
1 Tb butter
flour

Get all the trimmings left over from your fish after the dealer prepares it this way: Have the sea bass split and boned; the porgie and mackerel cleaned and boned. Some fish dealers don't like to spend any time with cheap fish like porgie and mackerel. If they won't bone it for you, take the fish whole and bone it after you boil it. (Traditional bouillabaisse is an obstacle course of bones, but I think there are really very few people who enjoy this kind of authenticity.) The lobsters should be alive and lively, the shellfish tightly closed.

At home, cut the bass into large slices about 1½ inches thick. If they are boned, cut each porgie or mackerel into

3 or 4 pieces. Wash and scrub the mussels with a wire brush. Scrub the clams and put them in the refrigerator. Lobsters, clams, mussels are quite safe to buy the day before. They can live several days in the refrigerator.

Boil up all the fish trimmings with the wine, water, bay leaf, thyme and peppercorns and simmer it for 30 minutes. Meanwhile, sauté the onions and garlic in olive oil in a heavy skillet. Crush the tomatoes and add them to the skillet. Strain the fish stock and return to a large pot along with the onions, garlic and tomatoes. Add monosodium glutamate and saffron, bring to the boil and simmer on medium heat for 10 minutes while you prepare the lobsters.

Kill the lobsters by plunging a knife into the thorax and splitting the lobster lengthwise. Discard the small sac near the head and cut up each lobster into about six pieces. Detach the claws from the second joints and crack them. Add to the soup. Next add sea bass and simmer for 10 minutes. Add porgie or mackerel and shrimp (in their shells, legs detached), simmer 5 minutes. During this last 5 minutes, steam open the clams and mussels in a little water over high heat. Work as much flour into a tablespoon of butter as it will absorb. Thicken the soup slightly with this by stirring it in vigorously.

Put a chunk of French bread into each large flat soup plate. Ladle on some hot soup and fish into the plates and decorate each with several clams and mussels. Be sure to have 4 or 5 loaves of French bread and pass extra baskets around with the soup. Serve a dry, white wine and provide some fruit and cheeses for dessert.

Despite the terrifying length of the directions, this bouillabaisse takes only about 45 minutes to prepare. It's a gorgeous meal for a large number of guests and costs just a bit over one dollar per person. It's good reheated but there's hardly ever a spoonful left over.

fish and shellfish

SHRIMP GUMBO

serves 4

Fresh okra is in season but since this vegetable is hardly known outside the South, you may have to use the frozen product. Traditional recipes call for long cooking but the flavor and texture of both shrimp and okra are much nicer with brief cooking.

1 lb fresh okra OR/
   1 pkg frozen okra
2 cups ripe tomatoes,
   peeled and chopped
1 onion, sliced

½ green pepper, sliced
1 bay leaf
1 sprig thyme
salt and pepper
1 lb shrimp

Sauté the onion and green pepper in a little olive oil. Add the tomatoes, herbs, salt and pepper and simmer all together uncovered for 15 minutes. Slice the okra in ¼-inch rounds and cook it for about 5 minutes in the tomato sauce. Peel and clean the raw shrimp, cut them in pieces if they are large and add to the pan. Simmer all together for 5 to 10 minutes. Serve with a bowl of white rice.

STEAMER CLAMS

serves 4

Any clams can be steamed but the best variety are known as "steamers" along the coast. They are smooth, thin-shelled clams that plump up to a tender juiciness rather like poached oysters. Unfortunately, they tend to be rather sandy. Soaking them in cold water into which you have thrown a large handful of cornmeal seems to help them disgorge some of the sand. Steamers should be well scrubbed with a medium stiff brush before cooking, since their broth is served along with them. People who like steamers will eat so many they will eat nothing else, so I always serve them as the main course. Allow 1 quart of steamers per guest. Remember, they're not getting anything else—unless you want to steam up some fresh summer corn on the cob to go with them and have a real orgy of eating.

4 qts steamer clams
½ lb butter, melted

Put an inch of cold water in the bottom of a large heavy pot or clam steamer. Distribute the clams evenly in the pot, turn the flame to high and cook, stirring them up from time to time. All should be open in less than 10 minutes. A clam steamer takes longer to open them and I can see no particular virtue in using one except that it's a great-looking pot with a spout on it for pouring off the juice. Lift out the clams with a slotted spoon (or you may tie them in cheesecloth serving bundles before cooking) onto hot soup plates. Carefully pour the broth through a cheesecloth-lined strainer. Serve individual cups of broth and melted butter to each guest. Medieval manners prevail so provide plenty of napkins.

fish and shellfish

PANNED WHITING

serves 4

Whiting is also known as merlan and hake in different localities. Its flesh is very delicate, white and lean; it is particularly suited to this rich, buttery cooking method. Flounder fillets cooked in this way are what you usually get when you order "Filet de Sole à la Meunière." If the whiting isn't strictly fresh, take flounder or something else that weighs from ¾ to 1 pound. Have the fish cleaned but the head and tail left intact.

4 whiting, about 1 pound each
salt and pepper
juice of ½ lemon

½ cup flour
½ to ¾ cup clarified butter
¼ lb sweet butter
chopped parsley and tarragon (optional)

Wash and dry the fish. Rub the cavity with a little salt and lemon juice. Dust them with flour and brown them in the clarified butter for about 4 minutes on each side. (Clarified butter is made by melting sweet butter, letting the milky sediment settle and carefully pouring off the clear butterfat. It will not smoke or burn as easily as ordinary butter. The flavor of good butter is of paramount importance to this dish and you cannot substitute any other frying medium.) Transfer the fish to a hot platter and season with salt, pepper and lemon juice. While you are frying the fish, let the ¼ pound of sweet butter brown slightly in a small pan. Stir it from time to time and take care that it doesn't burn. Sprinkle the fish with the herbs and pour the foaming brown butter over all.

Meats and Poultry

The garden, the lakes, and the ocean offer such interesting seasonal specialties that the juicy roasts and rich stews of winter should not be too much missed. The outdoor grill keeps us out of the kitchen and still satisfies the craving for a tender, rare steak or chop glistening in its own juices. Or does it? The city man's nostalgia for the rough and ready frontier days has resulted in more firelighter-flavored steaks than I care to remember. 'Tis the time of the hibachi, the self-turning spit . . . or maybe just a broiler rack propped on some old bricks. But all is not simplicity and charm. No subject seems to elicit more gratuitous advice or disagreement than the building, care and moment of truth of a charcoal fire. For years, ours were at the peak of cooking perfection approximately one hour after dinner was over. We usually had enough coals to barbecue a hog after we'd finished charring our lighter-fluid scented steaks. Just two coals deep for the surface of the food you are going to broil is really all that's necessary. The fire can be started with the coals in a pyramid, then raked out level when all are glowing well. A good thick layer of white ash should cover every coal; this is not likely to happen in less than an hour. It is possible to cook on the same bed of coals for a good two hours. For fish, poultry and vegetables, it is desirable to have had the coals burning at least that long, since these foods cannot be cooked over violent heat.

GRILLING STEAK

Whether for indoor or outdoor broiling, steak must be cut at least 1½ inches thick. This is assuming that you cook steak only to a succulent, juicy rareness. Sirloin and porterhouse, the most popular cuts, are almost impossible to ruin if the coals are properly prepared. Although it is not so luxurious, a shoulder steak, if cut from U.S. "prime" or "choice" beef can be delicious too. Shoulder is sold as "London Broil" in some localities. Flank, the long, lean flat muscle sold in a single piece, is the usual cut for London Broil. Except for this odd cut, as a general rule it is not wise to charcoal-grill very lean or small cuts of beef. Tenderloins (filet mignon) and club steaks are much juicier if they are pan-broiled in butter very quickly.

SHORT-CUT SAUCE BÉARNAISE

about 1 cup

In addition to glorifying various steaks, Sauce Béarnaise lends a gourmet touch to anything from spinach timbales to poached eggs or broiled chicken. Béarnaise is practically the same as Hollandaise except that it is strongly flavored with vinegar and tarragon. This recipe makes about 1 cup, enough for 4 people.

¼ cup wine vinegar
¼ cup dry white wine
1½ Tb fresh tarragon, minced
OR/ 3 tsp dried tarragon
½ cup melted butter
1 Tb minced scallions
or shallots
1 cup Blender Hollandaise
Sauce (See recipe)

Combine the vinegar, wine, tarragon and scallions in a small saucepan and reduce over high heat to about 2 tablespoons. Cool the mixture and beat it into the Blender Hollandaise with a wire whisk. Beat the melted butter by droplets into the Hollandaise Sauce. When the sauce is finished, add another tablespoon of minced tarragon.

meats and poultry

MARINATED LONDON BROIL

serves 4

Marinating breaks down the tough fibers of this almost completely fat-free (and therefore none too tender) steak. An average flank steak will serve 4 people amply.

MARINADE
½ cup olive oil
2 Tb soy sauce
½ cup red wine
salt and pepper
1 clove garlic, crushed

Mix all ingredients together and roll the flank steak in the marinade. Leave the steak in the marinade in a small, flat, covered dish for several hours at room temperature or overnight in the refrigerator. Turn it 2 or 3 times. Broil the steak on very high heat rather close to the coals, as this is a thin steak and overcooks easily. It MUST be cooked rare. Only a mountain lion could chew a well-done flank steak. Baste frequently with the marinade during the broiling period— not more than 5 minutes on each side. The grain of a flank steak is coarse and the meat will be very stringy if it is not properly carved. Lay the steak on a carving board and slice it diagonally holding the knife almost parallel with the carving board. Arrange the slices in the original shape of the steak on a heated platter and pour the juices that have accumulated in the well of the carving board over the sliced steak. London Broil is, like most steaks, especially good with Sauce Béarnaise.

OTHER THINGS TO GRILL

In the early part of the summer or vacation when the urge to cook everything out of doors is rampant, you might as well succumb to it. But there are a number of foods to consider other than the interminable steaks, hamburgers and frankfurters.

The Polish sausage, Kielbasy, is marvelous broiled over charcoal and served with chunks of fresh French or Italian bread. Green peppers, slices of eggplant brushed with oil, tomato halves, large mushrooms and parboiled onions all broil well on the coolish edges of the grill while the meat is cooking in the center. Chicken, baby lamb chops and whole fish are excellent cooked over charcoal and so are Italian sweet and hot sausages. Shish kebabs made with tender beef or lamb and vegetables can be assembled at home to bring to a beach party. Potatoes are delicious parboiled until almost done, then rolled in butter and roasted over a low charcoal fire to a golden brown. Jumbo shrimp marinated in soy sauce are an unusual treat for guests to broil at a cocktail party. The pyromaniac in all of us is dependable enough to plan a "grill your own" party with a variety of marinated meats, fresh vegetables or fish tidbits.

Spareribs are the only cuts of pork that seem to work out very well for charcoal grilling and even they must be parboiled to the tender stage. They can be done from the raw state but it takes forever and the coals flame up from the drippings. Pork chops get much too dried out and are better braised. Almost any kind of pork sausage with a casing is delicious grilled.

101

meats and poultry

CHARCOAL-GRILLED LIVER

serves 4

This is exquisite although it sounds like a shocking thing to do to calf's liver. Go to a quality butcher shop and be sure you get fresh calf's liver that has never been frozen. It's rather costly but since there is absolutely no waste, one pound of calf's liver will serve 4 people very well. Get through the fire-building business and let it burn down for at least an hour.

> *1 calf's liver steak (about 1 lb), cut 1½ inches thick*
> *¼ cup melted butter*
> *coarsely ground black pepper*
> *salt*
> *Sauce Béarnaise (See recipe)*

Brush the grill with salad oil. Brush the liver with melted butter and lay it on the grill. Sprinkle with pepper and salt. Broil about 5 minutes, then brush with butter, turn, and broil 5 minutes on the other side. Do not broil too close to the coals. The liver should brown but not get dry or rubbery on the outside. Brush with butter again before serving. Remove the liver to a hot platter and slice in ¼-inch slices. It should be just pink, but not really rare, inside. Serve with the Sauce Béarnaise, a good watercress salad and some home-fried potatoes. This deserves a good red wine.

GRILLED LEG OF LAMB

serves 6-8

This is such a favorite of my husband's and friends' I have shivered outside in the April chill of East Hampton to tend it on the hibachi. Leg of lamb prepared in this way has an utterly unrecognizable shape and flavor and it is somewhat like venison.

> *1 five to six lb leg of lamb*
> *2 cups dry red wine*
> *2 cloves garlic, crushed*
> *salt*
> *freshly ground black pepper*

Have the butcher cut along the lean, or underside of the leg and remove the bone. It should not be rolled. Spread it out flat and marinate it in the wine and garlic for a couple of hours at room temperature. Dry the meat, salt and pepper it and lay it on the charcoal grill, fat side down, and broil for 30 minutes. Turn it over and broil for another 15 to 20 minutes with the lean side down. It will have a rather burnt caveman roast look but never fear; let this misshapen thing rest for 15 minutes in a warm place before carving. Because it is of varying thicknesses, some of the meat will be well done (hopefully, not much), some medium and some medium rare. Carve it in slightly diagonal slices across the entire width of the meat. I serve an eggplant soufflé with this, but it *is* a bit of trouble and plain sautéed eggplant slices would be nice with it too along with an endive salad.

BROILED CHICKEN BREASTS WITH LIME JUICE

serves 4

Flying in the face of convention seems to pay off regularly when dealing with outdoor cooking. Orthodox methods of chicken grilling and roasting advise laving it in pounds of butter to prevent its drying out. But it will never develop a crisp skin if it is continually basted. A plump, fresh young broiler has plenty of fat in and under its skin and bastes itself. This has a crisp but tender skin and is a favorite even with people who don't ordinarily care for broiled chicken. Allow ½ chicken breast per person and a few extra if they are quite small.

> *2 broiler breasts, split (4 pieces)*
> *1 lime, cut in half*
> *salt and pepper*
> *tarragon (or Sauce Béarnaise)*

Wash the chicken and dry it well. Rub thoroughly with the cut lime, squeezing juice into the flesh. Salt and pepper. The charcoal fire should have burned for about 1½ hours. Brush the grill with a little oil and lay the chicken pieces on it, bony side down. Broil for 5 minutes. Turn and broil the skin side down for about 10 minutes. Pierce with a fork and if the juice runs clear yellow, the chicken is done. It should be golden and crisp, but not dry or overcooked. If the breasts are small, the skin side may take less than 10 minutes. Sprinkle with chopped tarragon or serve with Sauce Béarnaise (see recipe).

CHARCOAL-GRILLED VEAL KIDNEYS

I do all my outdoor cooking on a hibachi which has little draft doors that control the heat fairly well. But I suppose this will work just as well on any kind of grill. The fire should be quite hot as kidneys must cook quickly or they toughen. Buy 1 kidney per person. Wash the kidneys in cold water, dry them and cut each one into 4 slices. Remove the interior fat and white membrane completely. Brush the slices with melted butter, salt and pepper them and broil on a hot fire close to the heat for about 3 minutes on each side. Remove to a heated flameproof platter, pour ¼ cup of boiling cognac over them and blaze. Kidneys are usually served with a rice pilaf cooked in beef bouillon (see recipe).

GRILLED ITALIAN
SWEET SAUSAGES

serves 8

For picnics and Sunday brunches, Italian sweet sausages are a pleasant departure from the usual. They go very well with eggs and, as anyone knows who has ever bought one from a Greenwich Village vendor, are great with bread and peppers. Experience has taught me to allow 4 per person. They shrink a good bit during the cooking.

32 sausages (the "sweet" variety are hot and the "hot" ones are fiery)
1 cup dry red or white wine

Put the sausages in a heavy shallow pan (or you may have to use two large skillets) and pour in the wine. Pour in cold water to barely cover the sausages. Prick each sausage with a fork a couple of times and bring the liquid to a boil. Simmer, uncovered, for 15 minutes, skimming off any white foam that rises. Keep an eye on the sausages and if any start to strain at their casings, prick them again to prevent the skin from bursting. Drain them and set aside until 10 minutes before you wish to serve them. Broil over a medium low charcoal fire for 10 minutes, turning them to brown evenly.

STEAK AU POIVRE

serves 4

Many good things are quickly made and this is one of the most elegant there is. Choose your meat from a butcher who sells "prime" and "choice" beef that has been well aged. It is difficult to make this for more than 4 people at once.

*1 fillet steak about 3 inches
   across and 1½ inches thick
   for each person
whole peppercorns
1 Tb salad oil
salt*

*¼ cup bouillon
¼ cup cognac
1 Tb parsley, minced
2 Tb butter, cut in small
   pieces or softened*

Wrap a small handful of peppercorns in a dish towel and crush them with a hammer or heavy rolling pin. Pat some of the crushed pepper into each side of the fillets and let them rest at room temperature about an hour. Put the oil in a heavy skillet and let it get very hot but not smoking. Sauté the steaks about 5 minutes on each side for rare steak. Remove to a hot platter and sprinkle with salt. Pour off any fat that is in the skillet and deglaze the pan with the bouillon, scraping up the browned bits with a wooden spoon. Put in the cognac and boil over high heat a few seconds to evaporate the alcohol. Add the minced parsley and swirl in the butter. There should be a scant tablespoon of sauce to pour over each steak. In fancy restaurants Steak au Poivre is flamed at the table but that bit of showmanship is best left to the professionals.

CLUB STEAKS WITH
TARRAGON BUTTER

serves 4

This is a very simple, classic French way of pan-broiling beef steaks. Its success depends on your devoted attention for about 15 minutes and absolutely first-class meat. Please don't ask for *lean* club or Delmonico steak; nothing could be worse.

4 club steaks, cut about 1 inch thick

Trim all but ¼ inch of the firm white fat around the edge of the steak. Score the edges to prevent their curling. Melt a little of the trimmed suet in a heavy skillet. Sauté the club steaks in this hot fat for about 3 minutes on each side. Remove to preheated plates and place a dollop of tarragon butter on top of each one.

TARRAGON BUTTER

½ cup butter
1 Tb lemon juice
2 Tb minced tarragon or parsley and dried tarragon, mixed
salt and pepper

Cream the butter in an electric mixer or by hand, then beat in the lemon juice a little at a time. Beat in the herbs and seasonings with a wooden spoon. If the day is very warm, form it in 1-inch balls and chill in the refrigerator. Otherwise set the butter aside in a cool place to firm up slightly.

COUNTRY HAMBURGERS

serves 4

Admittedly not much beef cookery of note has proceeded from Southern recipes and the hamburgers in restaurants there rank among the worst in the world. But home-style hamburgers are juicy and flavorful. These not to be served on a bun, but with vegetables and salad.

*1½ lbs freshly ground
    chuck beef*
1 large onion, minced
¼ cup parsley, chopped

1 egg, beaten
1 slice day-old white bread
4 Tb butter
1 tsp salt
freshly ground pepper

Melt 1 tablespoon of the butter and sauté the minced onions until soft and transparent. Put them into a large bowl with the beef. Add the parsley and egg and beat with a wooden spoon. Trim the bread slice and crumble it into fine crumbs. Mix with the meat and about 1 teaspoon of salt and some freshly ground pepper. Shape into patties about ½- to ¾-inch thick and chill between layers of wax paper in the refrigerator. Melt the remaining butter over medium-high heat and sauté the hamburgers, taking care that they brown but do not burn. Three minutes on each side will cook them to the medium-rare stage. Serve the hamburgers with buttered noodles sprinkled with parsley.

MUSHROOM HAMBURGERS

serves 4

You can add almost anything you like to hamburgers provided you cook it first so that it amalgamates easily with the ground meat. I tried doing this without precooking the mushrooms and the bits of raw mushroom made the hamburgers fall apart. Serve these on thin slices of buttered hot toast.

½ lb mushrooms, chopped
butter
lemon juice
1 lb freshly ground chuck
   beef
1 egg, beaten
salt and pepper

flour
salad oil
4 slices buttered toast
¼ cup beef bouillon
2 Tb butter, softened
⅓ cup parsley, chopped

Sauté the mushrooms in a little butter and a squeeze of lemon juice. Mix with the ground beef, egg, salt and pepper. Form the mixture into four large patties, dust them lightly with flour and brown in a hot skillet filmed with salad oil. When they are cooked to the desired stage, lay each one on a piece of toast and quickly make the following sauce: Pour off any fat in the skillet and deglaze the pan with the bouillon (a spoonful of Madeira, cognac or red wine may be added at this time). Boil up the juices, scraping with a wooden spoon. When they begin to look sirupy (in about 1 minute), swirl in the softened butter and parsley and pour over the hamburgers. A spinach salad is quite nice with mushroom hamburgers.

HUNGARIAN STEAK PAPRIKA

serves 4

This is something like Beef Stroganoff but more interesting and unusual. The important ingredient is real Hungarian rose paprika which is never, but never, sold in supermarkets. It is quite cheap and will last for a year or so stored in an airtight container in the refrigerator or a cool place. Naturally, the fresher it is, the better it is. Paprikas Weiss, 1546 Second Avenue, New York City, is one of several places that sell a variety of fine paprikas and other spices. There is little point in trying to make this with anything but the best paprika since you must use a luxury cut of meat.

1½ lbs tenderloin beef
5 Tb clarified butter
juice of ½ lemon
1 cup heavy fresh cream
1 tsp Hungarian rose
paprika
salt

Have the butcher cut the tenderloin into ¼-inch slices. Brown the slices in the clarified butter very quickly, using 2 heavy skillets. Remove to a heated platter and keep warm. Deglaze one of the pans with the lemon juice and pour it into the remaining skillet. Add the cream and paprika and season with salt if needed. Pour the sauce over the sliced tenderloin and serve with buttered noodles or rice.

111

VEAL SCALLOPS

The little tender medallions or scallops of veal cut from the calf tenderloin are one of the most versatile cuts of meat known to cookery. The number of things done with them by Italian and French cooks is encyclopedic. We make breaded veal cutlets of them and pour tomato sauce on them. One of the reasons for this may be that American butchering techniques make it nearly impossible to get a properly cut veal scallop. It is easier to go to an Italian market than to try to explain the whole tiresome business to an American butcher. You can buy the whole "eye roast of veal" cut from the leg and slice your own in thin diagonal pieces. This cut also makes a beautiful, tidy little roast. Veal scallops have absolutely no waste and 1 pound serves 4 people.

VEAL SCALLOPS WITH BOURBON

serves 4

Find an Italian or French butcher or cut your own veal into slices about ¼-inch thick. Veal of this thickness must be very tender, first-rate meat.

> *1 lb fillet of veal, sliced*
> *4 Tb butter*
> *3 Tb bourbon*
> *½ pt heavy cream*
> *salt and pepper*

Dry the veal thoroughly; otherwise it will not brown. Dust it very lightly with flour. Heat the butter in a heavy skillet and when it is foaming put in the veal slices. Brown them quickly on both sides. Meanwhile, heat the bourbon, pour it over the veal and flame it over high heat. Lower the heat and stir in the cream. Season with salt and pepper and stir the sauce well until it thickens. Arrange veal on a heated platter and pour sauce over all.

VEAL SCALLOPS
WITH MUSHROOMS

serves 4

This is a Provençal dish that should be served with no other accompaniment than a green salad. It takes about 15 minutes to make. Ideally one should have the wood mushrooms that are called *cèpes*. I use canned Swiss mushrooms that are called *chanterelles* in French and *pfifferlinge* in German. They are available in gourmet departments of large department stores and in food shops catering to European trade. Fresh cultivated mushrooms may also be used but the flavor is quite different.

8 small, thin veal scallops	2 cloves garlic
2 Tb olive oil	½ cup dry white wine
1 can chanterelles, drained	4 small, ripe tomatoes,
OR/ ½ lb fresh	peeled and chopped
mushrooms, sliced	salt and pepper
½ cup parsley, minced	

Dry the scallops and brown them in hot olive oil very quickly. Remove scallops and cook the mushrooms and garlic in the same pan for a few minutes. Put in the wine and tomatoes and stir up the brown juices from the bottom of the pan. Stir and cook over medium-high heat for about 5 minutes. Return the scallops to this sauce and simmer all together for about 5 minutes. Season with salt and pepper and serve sprinkled with the parsley.

meats and poultry

SCALLOPINE ALLA MARSALA

serves 4

Since this dish must be prepared very rapidly and, once done, cannot wait, it is wise to restrict it to a few guests. Italians serve the pasta first, then the meat, but this would be a bit awkward for the cook-hostess. If you want to serve something like spaghetti with oil and garlic, bring it in after the meat course and no one here will be scandalized.

12 small, thin scallops of veal   *½ cup clarified butter*
salt and pepper   *3 Tb Marsala wine*
2 lemons, cut in half   *2 Tb beef or chicken stock*
flour   *or water*

Pound the scallops until they are almost transparently thin. Season them with salt, pepper and lemon juice. Shake them in a paper bag with a little flour, a few at a time, then shake them out so that only a thin film clings to them. Divide the butter between 2 heavy skillets and when it is very hot, sear the scallops very quickly on each side. Push the meat to one side and put ½ the Marsala and stock into each pan. Stir it around, scraping up the brown bits in the skillet. Spread the scallopine out in the sauce and simmer for 2 minutes. Serve immediately on heated plates.

VITELLO TONNATO

serves 12

Veal with tuna fish sauce is a classic Italian summer dish. It must marinate in its sauce for at least a day and is a marvelous party dish.

3½ lb fillet of veal
4 or 5 flat anchovy fillets
olive oil or butter
1 large onion stuck with
   2 cloves

1 bay leaf
1 carrot, sliced
pinch of thyme or sprig
   of fresh thyme
3 sprigs parsley

Tie the meat into a long, slim cylinder with kitchen string. Cut the anchovy fillets into small pieces and pierce them into the meat with the point of a small knife. Select a pan that the meat fits into rather snugly and brown the veal lightly in olive oil or butter. Put in remaining ingredients and enough cold water to half cover the veal. Cover tightly and simmer about 1 hour, turning the meat over several times. Cooking time will vary with the thickness and quality of the veal. When it is done, let the meat cool thoroughly so that you can cut it into thin slices. Lay it in overlapping slices in a long, narrow dish and cover it with the following sauce.

1 can tuna fish in oil (7 oz)
4 anchovy fillets
juice of 2 lemons
1 cup fine olive oil
2 Tb capers, drained

Pound the tuna fish and anchovies to a paste in a mortar or puree in a blender. Pound in the lemon juice and then the oil as if you were making mayonnaise. When the sauce is finished, add the capers and pour it over the veal. Cover the dish and marinate in the refrigerator for 24 hours. Serve cool, or at room temperature.

meats and poultry

HAM

There are an incredibly bewildering number of hams, both domestic and foreign, to choose from. They come raw, half cooked and fully cooked; hickory smoked, pepper cured, quick smoked, brine cured and canned.

Bayonne, Westphalian and Parma are the best of the imported hams. They are eaten "raw"—that is, they have been so thoroughly smoked and aged they require no further cooking and are simply sliced in paper-thin layers and served.

American country hams from Virginia, Kentucky and Tennessee are extremely fine and cost almost as much as the imported hams. If a ham has hung in the smokehouse long enough and is over a year old I don't see why it should be cooked either, but custom demands that we do so. Before cooking it keeps well for months in the refrigerator if you can spare the space. Country hams should be soaked for 24 hours in several changes of cold water and scrubbed vigorously with hot water and a stiff brush. The ham is then put on the fire in cold water to cover, brought slowly to the boil and simmered for about 30 minutes to the pound or until tender. A fine ham needs no cider, wine, bay leaf or any other spices in the cooking water. Most of all it certainly should not be debased by parading it out in the fool's dress of pineapple frills punctured with cloves.

When the ham is done, let it cool in its cooking liquor. Remove the ham when it is just tepid, skin it carefully and slice off the excess fat with a sharp knife until you have a smooth firm white layer of fat about ¼-inch thick over the surface. Ham is best served at room temperature or it may be chilled. It should be sliced as thinly as possible. Leftover ham keeps indefinitely in the refrigerator and is useful for many other dishes, sandwiches, salad, and for flavoring vegetables and soups. Ham is less likely to spoil if air circulates freely around it and if it is not cut off the bone until needed.

American meat packers are permitted legally to inject up to 10 percent of the ham's weight with water. I have bought some that should have been labeled "Ham Drink." There is no way of judging these precooked, processed hams except to beware of extreme wetness and mushiness. I find that some of the chain supermarkets have better hams of this type than those purveyed by the so-called luxury brands. Chain food stores do sometimes take the center cuts out of a whole ham and sell them for steaks; and the "half ham," whether butt or shank end, is minus its choicest part. If you can, pick out a whole ham and have the butcher cut it in half before your very eyes and you will be getting your money's worth.

I can't see much excuse for canned hams except for extended canoe trips or in localities where fire has not yet been discovered. Smoking preserves and flavors a ham. If it isn't smoked, it isn't ham. Canned hams taste like the brine they are cured in and the revolting jelly that generally comprises one third of the weight printed on the can.

The small, smoked ham butts sold in the supermarket are rather fatty but very tasty. They usually weigh less than 2 pounds and need only to be simmered about an hour. It's nice to have one in the refrigerator for sandwiches and nibbling.

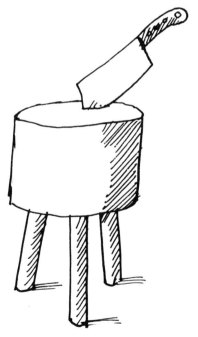

BRAISED HAM MORVANDELLE

serves 20

This is a French recipe that makes the most of a good plain mild-cured precooked ham, which may be bought anywhere. Most of the cooking can be done well in advance.

1 10-lb ham, precooked,
　　skinned and trimmed
3 Tb ham fat, melted
1½ cups sliced onions
1 cup sliced carrots
6 cups canned bouillon

1 Bouquet Garni: tie in a
　　cheesecloth bag, 1 bay
　　leaf, 8 peppercorns, 4
　　whole cloves, 6 sprigs
　　parsley, pinch of thyme
　　or branch of fresh thyme
4 cups dry white wine

Trim the ham and reserve enough fat to make the 3 tablespoons of ham fat melted down. Brown the onions and carrots in the fat and lay the ham, fat side up, on top of the vegetables. Put in the Bouquet Garni and the wine and bouillon. Cover and bring to a boil. Lower heat and simmer on top of the stove or in the oven (325° F.) for 2 hours. For top of the stove cooking, you will need a very heavy pot, preferably enamel-lined cast iron. In either case, baste the ham at least once every half hour. It is done when you can pierce it easily with a sharp kitchen fork. (The recipe may be completed to this point early in the day, then reheated.) The ham should rest at room temperature for 30 minutes before carving. The "Morvandelle" of the recipe is the following cream and mushroom sauce.

MORVANDELLE SAUCE

2 lbs mushrooms, sliced	3 cups ham liquid
5 Tb butter	¼ cup Madeira
3 Tb minced scallions or	2 Tb cornstarch dissolved
green onions	in a little water
salt and pepper	3 cups heavy cream

Sauté the mushrooms in the butter until lightly browned. Add the scallions and stir over the heat a couple of minutes. Season with salt and pepper. Set aside. Remove as much grease as possible from the ham liquid and boil it down rapidly to 3 cups. Add the Madeira, then stir in the cornstarch rapidly and continue stirring until it thickens. Add the cream gradually, stirring constantly, then add the mushrooms and onions and simmer for 5 minutes. The sauce should be rather thin and pale pink. Put the sauce in a warmed sauceboat and serve with the ham.

CHICKEN

I know that frozen chicken is status quo in supermarkets from Vancouver to Key West but I regard the freezing of chicken as mayhem. Europeans are forever complaining that "American chickens (among other things) have no taste, although they are attractive, etc., etc., etc." It's difficult to get chicken that someone hasn't thawed out in tepid water, draining it of all its juices and flavor. American poultry breeders have succeeded, for them almost too well, in producing some of the finest fleshed, plump chickens at the tenderest age, at the lowest price to be found anywhere in the world. Fresh poultry that has never been frozen (this is to disqualify "fresh frozen" chicken) costs a little more but it is still one of the most inexpensive of meats. It is also one of the most versatile and quick-cooking. There are very few people who don't like it, therefore it is an ideal choice for guests, provided it is not presented again and again in the same monotonous way. I have selected a few recipes that are neither too complicated nor too ordinary.

meats and poultry

POULET CHASSEUR

serves 4

This is chicken "hunter's style," a robust combination of fresh mushrooms, tomatoes and chicken flavored with cognac and white wine.

1 3-lb frying chicken	3 ripe tomatoes, peeled
flour	and chopped
½ cup clarified butter	½ cup white wine
1 small onion, chopped	2 Tb cognac
1 lb fresh mushrooms,	salt and pepper
sliced	2 Tb parsley, chopped

Have the chicken cut into 8 pieces. Dust it lightly with flour and brown it in the butter. Cover and cook until tender, about 20 minutes, and remove it to a warm platter. Add the onions and brown lightly, stirring with a spoon. Add the mushrooms and tomatoes and cook until most of the liquid has evaporated. Put in the wine and cognac and simmer a few minutes. Season with salt and pepper and return the chicken to the sauce to heat through. Serve sprinkled with the chopped parsley.

SOUTHERN-FRIED CHICKEN

serves 4

There is nothing unusual about Southern-Fried Chicken but it is unusual to get it properly done. It should have a crisp, dry crust, not a heavy, soggy coating of batter. Fried chicken should never be refrigerated but left to cool at room temperature if you want to serve it cold, but still crisp.

> 1 3-pound fryer
> 1 cup flour
> salt and pepper
> 1 qt peanut oil

Have the chicken cut into 8 pieces. Wash it and shake off excess water, but do not dry it completely. Put the flour with salt and pepper into a paper bag. Shake a few pieces of chicken at a time in the bag, remove them and press the flour into the chicken with your hands. Drop the pieces at once into very hot peanut oil. Start with the legs and thighs, then the breast pieces, and last the small bony pieces and wings. Drain on absorbent paper. Total frying time, 20 minutes for thighs and legs, slightly less for breasts, and 10 minutes for wings.

CHICKEN SAUTÉ

serves 4

This is a basic and simple way to cook chicken. It has a lovely, buttery flavor and juiciness, but must be served at once to retain those qualities.

1 3-lb fryer, cut into 8
   pieces
3 Tb clarified butter
salt and pepper
1 Tb fresh tarragon,
   chopped

2 Tb scallions, minced
½ cup dry white wine
½ cup clear chicken broth
   (canned)
2 Tb softened butter

Wash the chicken and dry it thoroughly with paper towels. You must use clarified butter otherwise it will begin to smoke and burn before all the chicken is browned. Brown the chicken on all sides in a heavy skillet, removing the pieces as they are browned and adding fresh pieces until all are finished. Season the chicken with salt, pepper and tarragon and return the dark pieces to the skillet. Cover and cook on low heat for not more than 10 minutes. Add the white meat and wings, baste all the chicken, cover and continue cooking for an additional 15 minutes. Pierce the leg to be sure it is tender and the juices run clear yellow with no tinge of pink. When it is done, remove to a hot platter and cover while you make this quick sauce: Drain off all but 2 tablespoons of fat and sauté the minced scallions in this. Add the wine and chicken broth, boil rapidly on high heat, scraping up the brown bits in the skillet with a spoon. When the liquid has reduced to about ⅓ cup, remove from the heat, stir in the softened butter, and pour the sauce over the chicken.

BONED CHICKEN BREASTS WITH MUSHROOMS AND CREAM SAUCE

serves 4

Boned, skinned chicken breasts are used for this luxurious dish. Since it is quite rich, nothing more than a green salad should be served with it and some fresh fruit for dessert. It must be made quickly.

2 fryer breasts, split, skinned and boned	*¼ cup chicken stock (canned)*
juice of ½ lemon	*¼ cup dry white wine*
salt and pepper	*1 cup heavy cream*
4 Tb butter	*2 Tb fresh parsley, minced*
½ lb sliced fresh mushrooms	*4 slices of dry white toast*

Heat the butter in a heavy skillet and add the mushrooms. Cook, stirring for 2 or 3 minutes. Dry the chicken breasts and put them in the skillet with the mushrooms, rolling them around to coat them with butter. Season with salt and pepper. Cover with a heavy lid and turn the heat quite low. After 6 minutes, press the meat with your finger. If it is firm and springy to the touch, it is done. Overcooking will dry and toughen these chicken fillets, but of course, be sure they are not pink inside. Lay one chicken breast on each of the slices of toast and prepare the following sauce. It only takes 2 minutes or so. Pour the stock and white wine and cook over high heat until sirupy. Stir in the cream and cook over high heat, stirring constantly until the sauce thickens. Fresh cream does not curdle when boiled. Taste the sauce and add a little more salt, pepper or lemon juice if needed. Pour the sauce over the chicken breasts, sprinkle with parsley and serve immediately. This may be served with cooked white rice in place of the toast.

123

Rice and Pasta

Rice and pasta are among the most versatile foods in the world and, since they keep indefinitely under almost any conditions, are an ideal base for the impromptu meal. What is nicer than linguini with fresh clam or mussel sauce, spaghetti carbonara or a saffron rice pilaf with shrimp, all of them effortless.

The rest of the world's peoples, except possibly for the English and the Irish, do not share our enthusiasm for potatoes. Therefore, with the exception of a few Southern dishes, most of the recipes are of foreign origin. The Italians make their splendid risottos, as do the French, the Spanish their national dish, Paella, and much of Oriental cookery is designed as a complement to the rice bowl.

Imported Italian long-grain rice or American converted long-grain rice is almost fool-proof and is essential to nearly every recipe that follows. The best utensil for cooking rice is a heavy cast-iron skillet with a cover. The reason rice is all too often a gummy mess is that it has been cooked in a deep narrow pot or has been cooked with more liquid than the rice can absorb. Long-grain rice cooks dry and tender in 20 minutes or less, thus obviating the use of "instant" rice which takes about 12 minutes to prepare.

Our admiration for pasta seems second only to that of the Italians, but that too is often overcooked. It should be "al dente"—"to the tooth," barely tender. All pasta is cooked in a large amount of rapidly boiling water. It must be boiling "like a volcano" in the words of an Italian friend, before the pasta is added.

There are quite a number of lighter, more interesting, things to do with pasta other than smother it under a heavy meat and tomato sauce. The famous Genovese "Pesto" is an aromatic basil and olive oil sauce delicious on spaghetti as well as on fish. The varieties of noodles and pasta manufactured in the United States are truly staggering, but the packages, excepting spaghetti, rarely give cooking times. The only way to determine when pasta is cooked "al dente" is by eating a piece from time to time during the cooking process. Fettuccine, for instance, cooks in about 5 minutes while cavatelli (shells) may not be done for 15 or even 20 minutes.

Although pasta is undeniably heavy, it is a quick, delicious summer meal when served with a light sauce and if the rest of the meal is compensatingly low calory.

SALSA AL PESTO

serves 4

The main ingredient of this sauce is a fine, fresh bunch of sweet basil. This is to serve on fish or 4 servings of pasta as a main course. Do keep pasta servings rather small because no matter how fine or delicate the sauce, mountains of pasta leave a leaden feeling. This sauce comes from Genoa, a city famous for its cuisine.

1 bunch fresh basil (about 1 cup of leaves)
1 clove garlic
6 - 8 pine nuts
2 Tb freshly grated Parmesan or Romano cheese
4 - 5 Tb olive oil

Pound the basil leaves with the garlic, nuts and a dash of salt in a mortar. Pound in the cheese, and when it is a thick purée, run in the oil as if you were making mayonnaise. The sauce should be very thick and creamy. It can also be made with parsley if basil is unavailable but it will have a completely different flavor.

rice and pasta

SALSA VERDE

serves 4

"Green Sauce" is made in much the same way as the above sauce but tastes more like a good French Dressing. It too can be used on boiled meat or fish as well as pasta.

1 cup parsley leaves	½ tsp salt
2 or 3 anchovy fillets	freshly ground black pepper
2 cloves garlic	juice of ½ lemon
	½ cup olive oil

Pound the parsley leaves, anchovies, garlic and salt in the mortar with the pepper and lemon juice. When it is a paste (this takes only a few minutes so don't panic), pound in the olive oil by droplets. This sauce could probably be made in an electric blender, but I have never tried it.

SPAGHETTI WITH CLAM SAUCE

serves 4

American clam sauce for spaghetti is usually made from large chowder clams, or quahogs. To prevent their texture from becoming like used tires, they are always finely chopped. This sauce is made with tiny, tender whole clams or mussels very briefly cooked and is, to my mind, immensely better. It is also immensely labor-saving since you neither have to pry open the clams, nor chop them.

4 servings of spaghetti	*½ onion, chopped*
3 qts little neck clams OR	*2 cloves garlic, minced*
3 qts mussels	*1 tsp flour*
½ cup butter	*½ cup clam or mussel broth*

Scrub the shellfish, put them in a pan with ½ cup water, cover and set them over high heat. Cook, stirring occasionally, about 5 minutes, until all are opened. Set aside shellfish and strain the broth through cheesecloth to remove any sand. Reserve ½ cup for the sauce and keep the rest to make Court Bouillon or soup. Melt the butter in a small, heavy saucepan. Simmer the onions and garlic in the butter until soft. Do not allow either the butter or the vegetables to brown. Stir in the flour (this thickens the sauce a trifle) and cook, stirring, 1 minute. Pour in the clam or mussel broth, and stir over medium heat a couple of minutes. Add the shelled clams or mussels and heat through. Toss with hot spaghetti or linguini and more butter if necessary. Strew a little minced parsley over the dish if you like, but cheese is never served with this. A light sprinkle of Italian crushed red pepper is nice for people who like a more spicy sauce.

PIZZAIOLA SAUCE

serves 4-6

Fresh tomatoes are the dominant flavor of this sauce, normally used to cover small steaks. A much better use for it is with pasta. You will be disappointed if you expect a rich, thick purée for the point of this sauce is the freshness of ripe, barely cooked tomatoes. It is a simple dish that will be appreciated by people who like plain spaghetti with butter or oil and garlic.

1½ lbs ripe tomatoes
¼ cup olive oil
3 cloves garlic, minced

salt and pepper
2 Tb fresh basil or 2 Tb
  parsley, chopped

Plunge the tomatoes into boiling water for a minute and peel them. Chop coarsely in a wooden bowl and do not lose their juices. Soften, but do not brown, the garlic in the olive oil over medium heat. Add the tomatoes, salt and pepper to taste and the basil or parsley. Simmer uncovered about 30 minutes. Stir the sauce occasionally to prevent scorching or sticking.

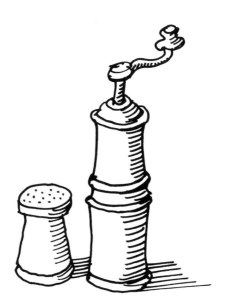

FETTUCCINE ALLA ROMANA

serves 4

A Roman chef created the original of this dish, simplicity itself, which numerous restaurants have been trying to complicate ever since. The myth that this is something occult is perpetuated by the waiter ministering to the pasta over a spirit lamp before your very eyes. ALL pasta has to be quickly tossed with its sauce and served immediately very hot! Unless you live in a castle, it doesn't matter whether you get the dish mixed in the kitchen or at the table. Fettuccine are egg noodles, the sauce is simply butter, cream and cheese. For 4 servings as a first course.

> *½ lb fettuccine, cooked and hot*
> *¼ lb sweet butter, melted*
> *½ cup heavy cream*
> *½ cup Parmesan or Romano cheese, freshly grated*
> *freshly ground black pepper*

Pour the butter and heavy cream over the fettuccine and mix gently. Mix in the grated cheese with a generous amount of pepper. Mix lightly but well in a hot dish. Serve on hot plates and pass more cheese at the table. The pasta must be hot enough to melt the cheese slightly.

SPAGHETTI CARBONARA

serves 4

Even bacon and eggs are combined with pasta by Italian cooks. Have whatever pasta you have chosen cooked, and very hot, when you pour on the sauce. Fettuccine or small macaroni are some other pastas to use this way.

4 servings of pasta
¼ lb double smoked bacon
3 eggs, beaten
3 Tb Parmesan cheese, freshly grated

Cut the bacon into matchsticks and fry it in a little butter until almost crisp. Drain off all but 2 Tb of fat, cool the pan slightly and add the beaten eggs to the bacon. POUR AT ONCE onto the hot pasta. The heat of the pasta should cook the eggs. Toss vigorously but be careful not to mash the pasta. Sprinkle with cheese and serve immediately. Pass more cheese at the table.

CANNELLONI I

My cannelloni is in no way to be construed as authentic. I have never been able to discover exactly what is authentic because it has never been served to me in the same way twice. The most marvelous cannelloni I have ever tasted was in Rome, probably because the noodles were home-made. Let no one deceive you; rolling out pasta needs the combined muscle power of a sculling crew. This is made with store-bought lasagna noodles, or large flat egg noodles about 3" x 4" if you can get them. Allow about 2 per person as a first course or 3 for a luncheon.

Lasagna or egg noodles,
   3" x 4"
1 lb ricotta cheese
½ cup melted butter

1 cup Parmesan cheese,
   grated
3 Tb fresh marjoram,
   minced
½ pt heavy cream

Cook the pasta according to package directions or until barely tender. Drain and spread each noodle with about 1 tablespoon of ricotta. Roll up, jelly roll fashion, and lay each noodle seam side down in a buttered baking and serving dish. Drizzle melted butter over all. Sprinkle with the grated Parmesan and marjoram. Pour the cream around the cheese-filled rolls of pasta. Bake in a hot, 400° F. oven 15 minutes. Baste frequently with the sauce in the pan to prevent the cannelloni from becoming dry and crusty. When it is golden, bubbly and hot through, serve immediately with more grated cheese passed at the table.

133

CANNELLONI II

This is an utter bastard in that it is not made with pasta at all, but with French crêpes (pancakes). Actually you may stuff the crêpes with any other filling you fancy and give it any name you like. Creamed spinach, mushrooms, minced chicken or veal are all very good alternates to ricotta for a change. The dish is made in exactly the same way as the first recipe except that crêpes are substituted for pasta.

BLENDER CRÊPES

1 cup cold water	2 cups sifted, all-purpose
1 cup cold milk	flour
4 eggs	4 Tb melted butter
½ tsp salt	plain salad oil

In the blender jar combine the water, milk, eggs and salt. Put in the flour and butter and blend on high speed for 1 minute. Cover the batter and let it rest in the refrigerator for 2 hours.

Rub a little salad oil all around a small, heavy skillet (or omelet pan) about 6 inches in diameter. Heat it to nearly smoking and pour in a bit less than ¼ cup of batter. Pick up the pan and roll the batter around to completely coat the bottom of the pan with a thin film. (These pancakes are more like tortillas than our thick breakfast pancakes; they should be almost paper thin.) Return to the heat and shake the pan back and forth over high heat about 60 seconds. Take the pan off heat and turn the crêpe by grasping the edge nearest you with the thumb and forefinger of each hand, OR/ flip it over with a toss of the pan, Voilà! and all that. The second side needs only a few seconds cooking and is not too attractive. Put the filling on this side. Slide the crêpe onto a plate and stack them up as you make them. Oil the skillet before making each crêpe. It does not matter if the crêpes get cold since they will be reheated in the baking stage. If you want to use the crêpes in some other way, place them in a single layer on a damp dish towel, roll it up gently and reheat in a 350° F. oven about 5 minutes.

Crêpes are an extremely useful thing to master. They can be used for hors d'oeuvres, the main course, or dessert, depending on what you care to fill them with.

Shrimp, lobster, crab or fish in a good cream sauce are excellent fillings. Leftover bits of ham, veal or chicken can be put to good use as crêpe fillings. Crêpes filled with cooked, chopped vegetables covered with a Sauce Mornay make a delectable luncheon dish. Dessert crêpes are perfect foils for summer's fresh fruits and berries (see Desserts).

RISOTTO OR PILAF

serves 4

Risotto and pilaf differ from plain white rice only in that the rice is cooked in a stock—chicken, beef, veal or fish—instead of plain water. Use whatever stock best suits the course the rice will accompany.

> 1 small onion, chopped
> 1 Tb butter
> 1 cup rice
> 2 cups boiling stock
> 1 tsp salt

Sauté the onion in butter until softened. Stir in the rice and cook until it looks slightly opaque. Converted rice becomes transparent first. Pour on the boiling stock, stir once around with a fork. Cover and cook over low heat about 20 minutes.

rice and pasta

PAELLA

serves 8

The Spanish national dish is made with or without: chicken, sausages, ham, garbanzos (chick peas), lobster, shrimp, scallops, clams and mussels. In Madrid, I have even had it served with tiny, purple fiddler crabs. It *always* is cooked in a good chicken stock, is flavored with saffron, decorated with red pimento strips and a few green peas, and has, as its chief ingredient, rice. My preference is for the seafood version, given here.

1 lobster, 1½ lbs or more	1 large onion, chopped
1 qt hard-shell clams (little necks)	½ tsp saffron
1 qt mussels	2 cups chicken stock
½ lb scallops	2 cups clam juice
½ lb shrimp, shelled and deveined	2 cups converted rice
2 oz smoked bacon, diced	small can pimentoes
	1 cup freshly shelled green peas

You will need a large heavy skillet plus a large, shallow oven-to-table casserole in which to bake and serve the paella. In Spain it is not baked, but Spanish cooks have a special paella pan and cooking device unavailable to American cooks. It may be cooked entirely on top of the stove if you are making only half the recipe, otherwise dividing all the ingredients between two pans is rather complicated. Preheat the oven to 400° F.

Either do it yourself or have the fish dealer kill the lobster, remove the sac near the head, and cut the lobster into pieces: the body in 4, the tail in 4, the claws cracked and separated from the second joints. You must cook the lobster right away once it is killed, so it is a good idea to learn to do the job yourself.

Put the bacon in a cold skillet and fry it slowly until crisp. Reserve. Sauté the onion and lobster in the bacon fat until onion is transparent and lobster turns red. Add the chicken stock, clam juice and saffron. Bring to a boil and add rice. Pour all into the shallow (3-inch deep) ovenproof casserole and cover with a double thickness of aluminum foil, tightly sealing the dish. Bake in a preheated 400° F. oven for 15 minutes. Remove foil and add the peas, shrimp and scallops but do not stir the rice. Re-cover with foil and return to oven for another 5 minutes. Meanwhile, put the clams and mussels in a pot with a little water and steam open over a brisk flame. Remove casserole from oven and add clams and mussels in their shells and decorate with strips of pimento. Bake uncovered another 5 minutes and serve.

Note: The rice should be tender and dry, each grain separate and all the seafood cooked through and hot. The total cooking time in the oven is 25 minutes, but if you allow the dish to cool off when adding ingredients, you may have to increase the baking time. It is advisable to eat a few grains of rice before adding the cooked clams and mussels. These must not be overcooked or they will be dry and tough. Just before serving, stir up the rice to distribute the seafood evenly.

Do not attempt to make paella in a deep, narrow dish or pan because the rice will be sticky.

Do not cook the mussels and clams directly with the paella. There is no way of gauging how much liquid they will release.

Do not use any rice other than American converted long-grain rice or imported Italian long-grain rice because it must cook tender in 20 minutes and absorb all the liquid. Short, stubby rice will be starchy and sticky.

VARIATIONS

CHICKEN must be sautéed to a golden color as the first step in the paella. Young chicken cut in serving pieces will be done in 20 minutes in a 400° F. oven.

HAM should be precooked, diced and sautéed with the onion.

SAUSAGES should be the hard, dry Spanish chorizos or Italian smoked sausages of the same type. Cut in slices ¼-inch thick and add to the paella with the rice.

GARBANZOS must be fully cooked (canned ones are), drained and added during the baking period with the rice.

CHICKEN AND RICE
WITH MUSHROOMS

serves 4

Quick and uncomplicated, even the dedicated non-cook can easily master this dish. It can be made more exotic by using distinctively flavored mushrooms such as cèpes or chanterelles. These usually come from France or Switzerland and are available in cans. Dried, Chinese black mushrooms are good too.

1 2½-lb fryer, disjointed	1 tsp salt
4 Tb butter	⅛ tsp fresh black pepper
1 small onion, chopped	½ lb mushrooms, sliced
1 cup rice	lemon juice
2 cups boiling chicken stock (canned)	chopped parsley

A disjointed chicken means that the breast is split, wings removed, wing tips cut off, legs detached from thighs and back cut into 2 or 3 small pieces, if used (usually the back, neck and giblets, except the liver, are stewed in advance to make the stock, then discarded). It does not mean hacked into 4 quarters on a buzz-saw, the economical (for them) but unesthetic way most supermarkets cut up chickens.

Wash and dry the chicken pieces thoroughly on paper toweling. Melt the butter and sauté the chicken until golden on all sides. Add the onions and sauté until transparent, 2 or 3 minutes. Drain off excess fat, if any. Add the rice, boiling chicken stock, and salt and pepper. Add the mushrooms which have been lightly browned in butter with a squeeze of lemon juice in a separate pan. Cover tightly and cook over low heat 18 minutes. Remove cover and test rice. It is done when you can bite through a grain easily but the rice is not mushy. All the liquid must be absorbed. If it is not, continue cooking uncovered over low heat until it evaporates. Sprinkle with parsley and serve very hot.

Note: This may be made in advance, then reheated, covered, in a moderate oven. In this case, the initial cooking period should be reduced by at least 5 minutes so that the chicken will not become dried out, nor the rice overcooked. *Chicken broth:* Either make your own with the neck, back and giblets, an onion, some celery and a little salt stewed together about an hour or use a good, clear canned chicken stock, undiluted. In either case it should be an aromatic, strongly flavored broth because the rice will be tasteless otherwise. Canned stock is improved by boiling it 5 or 10 minutes with a few sprigs of parsley, an onion and some celery tops to flavor and concentrate it. Make certain the stock is salted correctly.

HOPPIN' JOHN

serves 4

It isn't likely that everyone will fall into ecstasies over this but it is a novelty and may easily be adapted to other kinds of beans if you do not happen to be a black-eyed pea aficionado. In South Carolina it is served on New Year's Day and is supposed to bring good luck. Dried peas are commonly used, but fresh ones are better. Frozen black-eyed peas are available in any supermarket.

3 strips thick bacon, diced	*2½ cups water*
1 onion, chopped	*1 pkg frozen black-eyed*
1 cup precooked ham,	* peas*
* diced*	*salt and pepper*
	1 cup converted rice

Fry the bacon until crisp and remove. Drain off all but 2 tablespoons of fat and sauté the onion and ham in this for about 5 minutes. Add the water and when it comes to a boil, the frozen peas. Cover and cook 15 minutes over medium low heat. Taste for salt and sprinkle with pepper. Add the rice, cover tightly and cook on low heat for 20 minutes. The rice should be dry and fluffy, the peas tender. Be sure the peas are at least half done before adding the rice. If using dried peas or beans, they should be fully cooked. Crumble the reserved bacon and sprinkle over the. Hoppin'john.

rice and pasta

PICADILLO WITH RICE AND BEANS

serves 8

You need no special pots, foods or devices to make this Mexican dinner. You may have to hunt around a bit for cominos or cumin powder. Even if you can't get this spice it isn't a disaster—it just isn't quite as good. A dish of small red hot peppers is nice to serve with this.

1 Tb olive oil
1 clove garlic, crushed
2 cups cooked pinto or
  red beans
double recipe Risotto
  cooked with chicken
  stock
2 lbs lean, ground chuck
  beef

1 large onion, chopped
2 medium tomatoes,
  peeled and chopped
½ to 1 tsp cominos or
  cumin powder
salt and chili powder to taste
2 Tb capers, drained
4 Tb scallions, minced
1 hard-cooked egg, minced

In a heavy pot, heat the olive oil and crushed garlic together. Let stand a few minutes and remove garlic. You can leave it in if you like a stronger garlic flavor, but the beans are supposed to be quite bland. Put in the drained beans and cook over low heat, stirring with a wooden spoon from time to time to prevent sticking. They will gradually dissolve into an almost-smooth purée, ugly but good. Make the Risotto while the beans are cooking and begin the Picadillo: Sauté the ground beef in a little olive oil until crumbled and lightly browned (not hard or dried out). Add the onion and cook, stirring, 3 or 4 minutes. Add tomatoes and seasoning and cook, stirring occasionally until liquid has almost evaporated. Place in the center of a large, preheated platter and sprinkle with the capers, scallions and hard-cooked egg. Surround with the Risotto and serve the bean purée in a heated bowl. Corn bread and cold beer are delicious with this meal that definitely throws weight-consciousness to the winds.

JAMBALAYA

serves 6

One of many fine Creole dishes made with rice, jambalaya is a mouth-watering creation. I usually serve it to Europeans because it is a unique regional American dish. A large, shallow earthenware casserole is ideal for this.

3 chicken breasts, split
½ cup clarified butter
salt and pepper
¼ lb precooked ham,
    diced
1 large onion, chopped
2 cloves garlic, minced
1 large green pepper,
    sliced thinly
1 bay leaf
1 large sprig thyme, or
    dried thyme

1 small hot pepper,
    minced, or 1 tsp crushed,
    dried red pepper
1 lb tomatoes, peeled
    and chopped
3 cups chicken stock
1½ cups converted rice
12 Italian sweet sausages
    (this replaces spicy,
    homemade Southern
    pork sausages)
chopped parsley

Preheat oven to 375° F. Wash and dry the chicken breasts and brown them lightly in the hot, clarified butter. Sprinkle with salt and pepper and remove chicken. Put in the ham, onion, garlic and green pepper and cook until vegetables are softened, about 5 minutes. Add herbs, pepper and tomatoes and simmer all together until most of the liquid has evaporated from the tomatoes, about 10 minutes. Add chicken stock and rice, immediately stir a couple of times to mix ingredients. Place chicken breasts on top of rice and sauce, cover with double thickness of aluminum foil and place in oven on middle rack. Bake for 20 minutes, then test the rice and chicken. If not tender, bake a few minutes longer. Meanwhile, sausages should be cooked separately. Place them, in pairs, in a cold skillet and prick them with a fork. Cover with cold water and bring to a boil. Simmer, uncovered, 15 minutes. Drain, dry skillet and coat with a film of salad or olive oil. Sauté the sausages, turning to brown on all sides. When the jambalaya is done, decorate the platter with the sausages and some chopped parsley.

RED RICE AND BEANS

serves 4

Throughout the Caribbean Islands, Mexico and South America some form of rice and beans comprises a major part of the diet. Sharing the climate and economic conditions of these regions, many parts of the southern United States have their rice and beans dishes too. This is a combination of several local recipes.

½ cup smoked bacon,
   diced
1 large onion, chopped
2 cloves garlic, minced
3 very ripe tomatoes,
   peeled
1 cup (or more) chicken
   broth
sprig of sweet basil

1 tsp salt
1 Tb tomato paste
1 cup converted rice
2 cups cooked beans:
   garbanzos, white marrow
   or kidney beans, red
   kidney beans, pinto beans
   or California pink beans
2 Tb chopped parsley

Fry the bacon slowly in a heavy skillet until nearly done. Put in the onions and garlic, and sauté until soft. Chop the tomatoes and squeeze as much juice as possible out of them into a bowl. Add enough chicken broth to make 2 cups of liquid. Put the tomatoes, basil, salt, tomato-and-chicken broth into the skillet with the vegetables and bacon. Stir in tomato paste and bring to a boil. Add rice and cooked beans. Cover and cook over low heat until liquid has evaporated and rice is tender. Heat should be adjusted so that this takes 20 minutes or less. Turn into an earthenware casserole and sprinkle with parsley. This IS the main dish, but you may also serve some ham, chicken, fish or shellfish with it if you like. Pass some hot pickled peppers with it.

Vegetables

With the truly fresh vegetable headed for the fate of the dinosaur except in remote, backward countries, there is all the more reason to accent its fleeting pleasure in summer meals.

In the provinces of France, family outings are organized on Sundays when everyone piles into the ancient Citroën to drive to a certain small country restaurant where the specialty is fresh asparagus! I wish I knew *one* in the state of New York that serves fresh peas. Alas, the Jolly Green Giant has nearly every pea patch in his mammoth grip.

Garden peas braised with lettuce and tiny onions deserve to be served, with fanfare, as a separate glorious course. Tiny string beans picked at their peak of flavor, tossed with a lemon and egg sauce, eggplant and zucchini cooked in a Provençal ratatouille, or asparagus dressed in a golden Hollandaise, are Olympian dishes not to be treated as mere frills.

Frozen vegetables are, on the whole, an enormous improvement over canned ones. But for all their "fresh-frozen" and "picked at the peak of perfection" hoopla, they will never, never taste like vegetables picked and served the same day. One really doesn't know whether to laugh or to cry upon reading Joseph Wechsberg's account* of a conversation with a famous Hungarian restaurateur, Charles Gundel, who said, "My son, Charles, sends me menu cards from New York, where, it seems, they use the word fresh with everything. . . . I am told, 'fresh' does not necessarily mean fresh in America. Here, (in Budapest, 1948) when we say 'fresh,' we mean, of course, vegetables that are served the very same day they come out of the garden . . ."

Any general cookbook gives adequate instructions for the cooking of fresh vegetables. The important thing to study is how to choose good produce. James Beard's basic cookbook in paperback published by Dell does an explicit and thorough job of explaining how to recognize fresh or poor vegetables and what quantities to buy.

---

* *Blue Trout and Black Truffles,* Alfred A. Knopf, Inc., 1953.

BRAISED SPINACH

serves 4

Presumably everyone has some method of cooking spinach. But, since frozen spinach, because of its availability and cheapness, has all but obliterated fresh spinach, I offer this recipe to remind you of how amazingly good this much-maligned vegetable can be.

2 lbs young, fresh spinach	¼ cup melted butter
1 tsp salt	2 hard-cooked eggs, shelled
⅛ tsp freshly ground pepper	lemon wedges

Wash the spinach by lifting and swishing it through 3 changes of cold water, leaving the sand at the bottom of the sink each time. Do this even if the spinach is said to have been "pre-washed." Discard large, tough or blemished leaves. Break off the stems with a slight pull upward to remove some of the spine of the leaf. Put the spinach in a large, heavy pot, cover and cook in the water that clings to the leaves over medium heat. It will reduce from what seems like a bale to a few cupfuls in a matter of minutes. When tender, drain thoroughly and toss in the hot pot with salt, pepper and melted butter. Serve in a heated dish decorated in the old-fashioned way with slices of hard-cooked egg and wedges of lemon.

CREAMED SPINACH

serves 4

Cook fresh spinach as in preceding recipe. Drain well and chop roughly. When it is cold, add it to the following sauce.

2 lbs cooked spinach
1 Tb butter
2 Tb onions, minced

vegetables

SAUTÉED ZUCCHINI OR YELLOW SUMMER SQUASH

serves 4

I know of no better vegetable to serve with charcoal-broiled fish. This is light and delicate in flavor and quickly prepared.

2 lbs zucchini or
  yellow squash
2 Tb butter
1 Tb oil

juice of ½ lemon
salt and pepper
2 Tb chopped parsley

Wash and dry the vegetables, but do not peel. Slice in ⅛-inch rounds. Heat the butter and oil in a heavy skillet until foaming. Put in the vegetable and sauté gently until tender and transparent, but not mushy and shapeless. Turn frequently with a spatula and cover part of the cooking time. When it is done, in 15 to 20 minutes, squeeze on the lemon juice, season with salt and pepper and sprinkle with the parsley. Turn into a heated dish. Zucchini may be served cold as well, but yellow squash is better hot.

RATATOUILLE

serves 6

A Mediterranean mélange of summer vegetables, this is exquisite served hot or cold. It may be a separate course and it makes a marvelous dish for the buffet table. It takes time to prepare, but is even better when reheated. If there is any left over, ratatouille makes a flavorful filling for omelets.

½ lb zucchini
½ cup olive oil,
    approximately
1 medium eggplant
2 cups yellow onions,
    sliced
2 green peppers, cut
    in strips

2 cloves garlic, minced
1 lb red, ripe tomatoes,
    peeled
salt and pepper
3 Tb minced parsley and
    basil, mixed

Wash the zucchini, dry it and slice it in ⅛-inch rounds. Put a little oil in a heavy skillet and begin sautéeing the zucchini a layer at a time, then removing it to a side dish. Peel and slice the eggplant in the shape of French fried potatoes. Add more oil to the skillet and sauté the eggplant, then place it in the dish with the zucchini. Add more oil and sauté the onions, green peppers and garlic until softened. Cut the tomatoes in half and squeeze out the juice and seeds. Chop them and add to the vegetables in the skillet. Season with salt and pepper and cook, uncovered, until the juice from the tomatoes almost evaporates. Stir frequently. Return the eggplant and zucchini to the skillet with the other vegetables. Adjust salt and pepper, sprinkle with herbs and cook, covered, over low heat about 5 minutes. Uncover and cook over slightly higher heat another 15 minutes, lifting the vegetables and turning carefully with a spatula until nearly all the juices have evaporated except for a few tablespoons of richly flavored oil. Set aside, uncovered, until serving time, then reheat slowly or serve cold. It is important for each vegetable to retain its own texture and flavor. Be careful not to overcook. By "cold" I mean at room temperature. Refrigerating diminishes the flavors too much.

BRAISED PEAS À LA FRANCAISE

serves 4

The ultimate in fresh garden peas, these are worthy of being presented at court—and they were. In the court of Louis XIV eating this delicacy became as chic with the ladies as eating nothing is today in America. Only very young, tender peas shelled just before cooking should be used. It would be ridiculous to serve this dish except as a separate course with a chilled, fairly dry white wine.

1 large fresh head	*2 bunches scallions*
Boston lettuce	*6 Tb butter*
3 lbs fresh, tender	*½ cup water*
green peas	*1 Tb sugar*
10 sprigs parsley	*½ tsp salt*
freshly ground black pepper	

Wash the lettuce, discard outside or wilted leaves and cut the head into 4 wedges. Tie with white kitchen string into small bundles. Shell the peas and tie the parsley in a bunch. Trim the scallions and cut off tops so that only the bulbs, about ¾-inch, remain. In a heavy enameled skillet or saucepan, bring 4 tablespoons of butter, the water, sugar, salt and pepper to the boil and put in the peas. Shake the pan to coat the peas. Lay the parsley on the peas, then the scallion bulbs and finally the lettuce bundles. Cover with a heavy, domed lid or an inverted shallow bowl so that the condensed steam will fall back on the vegetables. Braise over very low heat about 20 minutes. Remove the cover and shake the saucepan occasionally so that the vegetables cook evenly. When the peas are tender, the cooking liquid should have nearly evaporated. Remove the parsley and lettuce. Toss the peas and scallions with the remaining 2 tablespoons of butter and arrange the servings on 4 heated plates. Remove string from the lettuce and garnish each plate with one wedge. Discard the parsley.

PARSLIED NEW POTATOES

serves 4

Another lovely vegetable that really deserves the diner's full attention is a dish of tiny new potatoes. Buy the small shiny, pale beige potatoes. The red ones are dyed for some unaccountable reason. I guess it's like green carnations; some people prefer improbable colors to natural ones.

2 lbs small, whole new potatoes (not more than 2 inches in diameter)	1 Tb salt
	2 Tb butter
	freshly ground pepper
2 cups water	3 Tb parsley, chopped

Scrub the potatoes under running water with a soft brush. Boil them in their jackets in the salted water until just tender, 15 to 20 minutes. Drain, put them back in the pot and shake over low heat to evaporate excess moisture. Put in the butter and shake the pot to coat all the potatoes evenly. Brown them lightly over low heat. Just before serving, grind on pepper and sprinkle with the parsley.

149

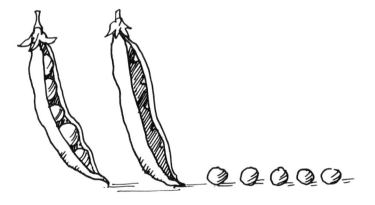

vegetables

SAUCE BÉCHAMEL
(CREAM SAUCE)

2 Tb butter	½ tsp salt
2 Tb flour	⅛ tsp pepper
1 cup boiling milk or	nutmeg
light cream	

Before starting the standard Béchamel recipe, melt 1 tablespoon of butter in a heavy saucepan and gently cook 2 tablespoons of minced onion in it. Do not brown. Add the 2 tablespoons of butter and melt. Stir in the flour and cook, without browning, for 2 minutes, pour in the boiling milk or cream and cook, beating rapidly with a wire whisk until sauce is smooth and thickened, about 3 minutes. Off heat, add salt and pepper and grate in a little nutmeg. Preheat the spinach in this sauce. (If the spinach is still hot when added to the sauce, it overcooks.) This is good as a filling for crêpes (see recipe) as well as an ideal accompaniment to fish or veal. Creamed spinach is a fine base for poached eggs sprinkled with grated Parmesan and run quickly under a hot broiler to glaze.

GREEN BEANS WITH EGG AND LEMON SAUCE

serves 4

The kind of slender, immature beans needed for this dish are almost an oddity, but if you have a garden this is another way to enjoy the brief season of early summer vegetables. The beans should be picked when they are about ¼-inch in diameter and about 3 inches long.

> *2 lbs tiny, whole green beans*
> *2 eggs*
> *juice of 1 lemon*
> *3 Tb melted butter, slightly cooled*

Trim just the tips of the beans and drop them in boiling salted water. They should still be green, slightly crunchy but tender in 8 to 10 minutes. Test by eating one after 7 minutes of cooking. Drain and keep hot. Reserve ½ cup of the bean liquid. Beat the eggs and lemon juice together with a wire whisk until frothy. Add the butter and a few spoonfuls of the bean water whisking rapidly over low heat until the sauce thickens. Pour over hot beans and serve at once.

TIMBALE D'AUBERGINE

serves 4

If I called this "eggplant custard," who would eat it? That's what it is but the French name suits the elegance of this dish inspired by both French and Italian cookery. Very good with roast meats or broiled steaks and chops.

2 medium eggplants
  (about 6 inches long)
1 tsp salt
2 Tb olive oil
1 clove garlic, minced

3 eggs
1 cup milk or light cream
½ tsp salt and ⅛ tsp pepper
½ cup Parmesan cheese,
  freshly grated

Peel the eggplants, slice them and sprinkle with the salt. Leave them to drain for half an hour. Dry the slices and gently simmer in the olive oil until most of their moisture has evaporated. Purée the eggplant by pressing it through a sieve and combine it with the garlic, eggs, milk and seasonings. Pour into a well-buttered 1½-quart soufflé dish or casserole. Sprinkle with the grated cheese. Set in a pan of hot water and bake in a preheated 350° F. oven until set, about 30 minutes. Serve immediately.

Cheeses

Wine and cheese are indisputably ideal companions. But gin and cheese, although rather incompatible, are nonetheless a fact of American summer social life. Those monarchs of cheese, Brie and Camembert, both taste terrible with liquor. They should always be served at the end of a meal when available; they are both at their best during the winter months, though. In assembling a cheese tray for a cocktail party, it is best to stick to the utterly bland or the distinctively flavored cheeses.

Choosing cheeses is a tricky business. It requires a keen eye, sharp nose, probing finger and a lot of gall. If you don't know what you're supposed to be looking for, *The Cheese Book* by Vivienne Marquis and Patricia Haskell has recently been published by Simon and Schuster. This outline deals only with a few general rules and suggestions for cheeses to serve for summer entertaining.

When you buy cheese, be sure the place has a fairly rapid turnover and a reputation for reliability. Beware the picturesque small shops offering 101 varieties. They can't possibly maintain a stock in peak condition. The soft, ripened cheeses are generally in their prime only three or four days. After that they become sticky, ammoniated and bitter. Domestic Camembert is standard winter and summer and is a safer bet during the summer months when the real thing is out of season.

CREMA DANICA is a recently developed Danish cheese that has many of the qualities of Brie. Its creamy, delicately flavored center is pale yellow and the rind is pure white. Crema Danica comes in 6-ounce bars and, like nearly all cheese, should be served at room temperature. It is best for dessert.

TRIPLE CRÈME PARFAIT is one of a number of brands of imported super-fatted creme cheeses. It is a small, round cheese with a streaky orange crust and rich, custardy center. Its paper wrappings should be clean and fresh, never brown, sticky or smelly. Le Roi and Boursin are some other good brands of triple creme cheese. All should be ripened at room temperature 6 or 7 hours before eating. Dessert only.

AMERICAN CREAM CHEESE is an excellent buy and besides being good all by itself, takes very well to various herbal flavorings. Don't hesitate to serve it with toasted crackers either before or after dinner.

PONT-L'ÉVÊQUE is one of the most celebrated French cheeses and can be found in almost any good cheese store. It is a square, golden, soft-crusted cheese with a much stronger smell than taste. It is better to buy this a bit under-ripened and let it come to maturity at home. Overripe Pont-l'Évêque is just disgusting. Don't touch it if the paper is sticky or has dark blotches. This cheese can hold its own with strong drinks, although it's best with red wine.

PORT-SALUT is also called Port-du-Salut and sometimes, St. Paulin. Many different versions are made in France. The French Port-du-Salut imported here is under the "Abbey" label. Its flavor and aroma are rather mild. The Danish Port-Salut is considerably stronger, and so are some sold as St. Paulin. Although some people may be driven from the house, fans of robust Port Salut are fanatical.

CANADIAN CHEDDAR is considered closest to the genuine English cheddar. Since our cheese industry has succeeded in barring the import of English cheddar, the Canadian is, il-logically, the one you must look for. It should be aged and cut from large wheels. This cheese is pleasant to nibble all by itself or with white bread and sweet butter.

AMERICAN CHEDDAR, whatever this is. Cheeses with vaguely cheddar flavor may be anything from a pumpkin orange Texas longhorn to the nearly white Vermont variety. My favorite is New York State cheddar, whether young, middle-aged or old. New York's Herkimer County cheeses are prized among cheddar lovers.

cheeses

COON CHEESE is a pale yellow, sharp type of domestic cheddar that is very good and reasonably easy to come by in supermarkets. This is a reliable "drinker's cheese."

Note: Bitterness is the chief flaw in some aged cheddars. It comes through most strongly in the aftertaste. Utter taste-lessness is the main characteristic of some of our 60-day-wonders (the minimum aging time for nonprocessed, or, "natural" cheeses). The only way to discover these faults is by tasting the cheese. The dealer who won't let you sample a sliver isn't worthy of your trade.

EMMENTHAL, or Emmenthaler, is the real name of Switzerland Swiss. Many other kinds of cheese are made in Switzerland and Emmenthal is made in many other countries. "Imported Swiss" means nothing. If you are paying for it, be sure you get genuine Emmenthal made in Switzerland; sometimes it is stamped "Switzerland Swiss." Descendants of Swiss settlers in Green County, Wisconsin, produce an excellent authentic nut-sweet Emmenthal in the time-honored manner. Always buy from a wheel cheese.

GRUYÈRE, made on both sides of the Jura Mountains that divide Switzerland and France, is a splendid cheese similar to Emmenthal. But it has much smaller holes and a brownish rind. French Gruyère has a slightly sharper and, to me anyway, better flavor than the Swiss version. It is delicious eaten alone and useful in cooking. It melts and grates well and is irreplaceable in a classic Swiss Fondue.

ROQUEFORT, a blue-veined white sheep's milk cheese, is often imitated but never duplicated. This unique cheese is protected by law in France and none may be exported under the name except that aged in the limestone caves of the Roquefort district of Causses. Roquefort should look moist and fresh, not dry or discolored and chalky. Taste to be certain it is not too old or too salty and buy only from quality stores with a fast turnover.

AMERICAN AND DANISH BLUE are much fatter and more buttery than the more astringent Roquefort. Both are densely blue-veined, strong flavored, and made from cow's milk. They are competitive in price. A domestic blue is preferable to an over-the-hill import oozing in its sticky wrapper. Either should be unwrapped and ripened at room temperature for several hours.

GORGONZOLA, the famous Italian veined cheese, travels well and invariably arrives, and is sold, in good condition. Rich and creamy, it is marbled with green, rather than blue, veins. Deservedly popular, it is difficult to go wrong with this cheese.

CHÈVRE is the generic term for cheese made of goat's milk. These cheeses are tiny and expensive, even in France. Little known to Americans, chèvres are an acquired taste in any country. Goat's milk produces a dry, strong, tingly tasting white or grayish cheese. It is quite salty and usually comes in a small pyramid or cylindrical shape 2 or 3 inches in diameter. Wrapped in chestnut leaves and tied with grass thongs, even a young (1 or 2 months old) chèvre lends an earthy touch to the cheese tray. Valençay is a reputable pyramid-shaped chèvre and Le Banon is a delicious brand that comes in a small, round, flat cake. True "goat" connoisseurs revel in the biting, rasping flavor of a year-old chèvre that looks and smells as though it had just been dug from a rich compost heap. I have found that the young chèvres imported here have little flavor until they ripen at room temperature for a day or two.

FETA is the gift of the Greek goats. It is a pressed white cheese that looks freshly made but has actually been preserved in a saltwater brine. It resembles, but does not taste at all like, our farmer's cheese. Feta is good sprinkled with paprika or thyme and eaten with hot peppers or Greek olives. Greek and Italian grocers carry this cheese.

PROVOLONE, a smoked Italian cow's milk cheese, has some of the characteristics of goat cheese. Its salty, smoky flavor is fine with most alcoholic beverages and this cheese is easily found in Italian neighborhoods.

PECORINO ROMANO is a cheese I always keep on hand to grate over pasta. It keeps indefinitely if stored in a plastic box in the refrigerator. Romano is a hard, salty cheese that should be shaved off in thin slices and served on buttered dark bread.

LIEDERKRANZ, despite its Germanic name, is a native American. Its incredible odor comes enclosed in a small oblong box and a soft orange rind. Fortunately, the paler, glossy interior of this cheese is much milder than its aroma. It should be served fully ripened; otherwise the flavor is enormously distorted. Most supermarkets carry Liederkranz and its makers stamp the box with the final date on which it can be sold. They do the same for their Camembert and therefore both are reasonably safe buys.

LIMBURGER, long the synonym for stinky, is, nevertheless, a great favorite of many Americans. It has been produced here for a long time and is still imported from Germany too. The domestic Limburger is probably more reliable than the imported unless you are really certain of your selection. Its rambunctious aroma and flavor are best appreciated with onions, beer, and dark, rough breads.

BIERKASE is literally "beer cheese," originally from Germany. Why anyone wanted to I don't know, but it has been exactly duplicated by Wisconsin cheese makers. This firm, pale yellow loaf cheese looks innocuous enough but its rather acrid flavor is strictly for strong stomachs.

ALSATIAN MUNSTER is highly regarded in France where I first encountered it. When it is exactly à point, it leaves the uninitiated pale and faint. Despite its penetrating smell, a proper Munster's soft, creamy interior is far milder than one would suspect. It is difficult to find, but would be a gourmet treat to those with a predilection for strong cheese. Obviously, the pale, nearly tasteless, waxy American Munster bears not even the slightest resemblance to its European forebear.

PROCESS CHEESES. As though we did not perpetrate a great enough crime by creating those wretched masses of orangy, plastic-textured "cheeses," we are even importing some of them from the European countries that have imitated American methods. Process cheeses, foreign or domestic, are an insult to the most naive palate. Except in aircraft survival kits, there seems to me to be little excuse for them.

159

cheeses

Desserts

True epicures are loath to spend their calory allowance on desserts, especially when everyone is suffering from summer exposure. Berries, melons and fruits are a light and appropriate ending for most summer meals if one cannot be content with cheese. When there are many guests and a dessert is really expected, I am fond of molded desserts, for instance, Coeur à la Crème, that can be made early in the morning or even the day before. To be frank, there are cooks and there are bakers and I make my stand in the first category. Rich pies and cakes are part of our culinary heritage and very good they are too—but I associate them with roaring ranges and winter naps to sleep off their soporific effect. No child will agree with my point of view, but then, most of them will take a fig newton over Baba au Rhum any day. So let 'em eat cookies, I say!

Mixes made cake-making a snap and now granny's place in the kitchen has been almost totally usurped by a sweet little old frozen baked goods farm. Some of the frozen pies ready to pop into the oven are of very good quality. Most of the fully cooked frozen cakes are acceptable even though they are hideously sweet to my taste buds. I don't know where it all started, but the sweetness of American desserts is matched only by those of the Middle East. French desserts derive their luxurious character from the butter, cream and eggs so lavishly employed in them. We, on the other hand, seem to have confused richness with sweetness and almost any American recipe can be improved 100 percent by reducing the sugar by 50 percent.

Before my cook's apron is torn off by an indignant patriotic organization, let me hasten to add that no one appreciates more than I do a fine, dry, flaky American pie crust filled with fresh fruits or berries. Also, one of the few points of dissent I have with the superlative English cookbook author, Elizabeth David, is that while the Italians took ices to America, "the Americans have brought them back to Italy transformed out of all recognition into monstrous schoolboy treat, an outsize slab of iced pudding made of heaven knows what nauseous sham creams and essences and gaudily bedizened with false colors. Cloying and sickening, they lie upon the stomach like some abominable sodden sponge."* I don't know what American ice cream manufacturer could be engaged in this Coals-to-Newcastle operation, although there is certainly cheap American ice cream that fits Mrs. David's description.

Our quality brands and some small, local dairies put out excellent ice cream made with fresh cream and fruits and containing no artificial colorings. The sweetness is always a bit excessive for sophisticated tastes but I suppose we shall just have to bear with that failing until someone brings out a brand "For Adults Only." Until then, good quality ice cream is a lovely summer dessert, especially when it is given a tart freshness with a spoonful of fresh, *unsweetened,* crushed berries or fruit. I don't approve of pouring sweet liqueurs over ice cream; it only accentuates the negative.

Fresh fruits and berries, which have no sugar added, are delightful flavored with a drop of kirsch, framboise, cognac, dry rum or bourbon. Kirsch, a distillation of cherries, has a special affinity for fresh cherries as well as a mixture of fruits. Framboise, an eau de vie distilled from raspberries, may be used to advantage with almost any fruit or berries. Bourbon and cognac are both nice on peaches and apricots. A few drops of rum lend a pleasant taste to whipped cream to be served with fresh strawberries.

163

FRESH FRUITS IN KIRSCH

Choose an assortment of oranges, apples, fresh cherries, melon balls and peaches. Peel and slice the larger fruits and put them in a bowl with enough kirsch to flavor them and leave them to macerate in the refrigerator until serving time.

* *Italian Food,* Alfred A. Knopf, Inc., 1958.

DESSERT CRÊPES

These are very easy to make, can be cooked in the morning and assembled at serving time. Crêpes make an excellent background to the flavors of summer fruits and berries. Procedural instructions are the same as for the crêpes used in Cannelloni listed in the Index. The batter is a little different.

THE BATTER

¾ cup cold water
¾ cup cold milk
3 egg yolks
6 Tb melted butter

3 Tb rum or cognac
1½ cups sifted all-purpose
flour

Combine all ingredients in the blender jar in the order listed and mix at high speed for 1 minute. Cover the batter and let it stand in the refrigerator for 2 hours or longer. Dessert crêpes should be fried in clarified butter rather than salad oil. Put the filling on one half of the crêpe and fold the other half over it like an omelet.

APPLE. Make some fresh applesauce, flavor it with a little Calvados and serve with unsweetened whipped cream.

APRICOT. Cook some fresh or dried apricots with a little sugar and brandy and enough water to keep them from sticking, about 20 minutes. When most of the liquid has evaporated, spread the apricots on the crêpes and roll up. Sprinkle with pulverized sugar and run under the broiler a moment to warm them and brown the sugar slightly.

BERRIES. Strawberries, raspberries, blueberries and blackberries all make wonderful fresh fillings for crêpes. Sprinkle the berries with a little kirsch or framboise and leave them to macerate for about an hour at room temperature. Put a spoonful on the first third of the crêpe, roll them up and serve with unsweetened whipped cream. Allow 2 per person.

CHERRIES. Fresh cherries must first be stoned. This not only makes work, it is wasteful. A bowl of plump, dark red cherries needs no crêpes. A good brand of cherry jam is a fine filling for crêpes. Spread it on, roll up the crêpes and brush with melted butter. Sprinkle with sugar and heat the crêpes under a low broiler. Warm some kirsch and flame them at the table.

PEACHES AND PLUMS. Peel the peaches and stone them. Plums do not need peeling. Stew them gently in a very little water with a bit of sugar, *if necessary*. Flavor with Cointreau and when the fruit has cooked to a thick mass, put a spoonful on each crêpe and roll up. Sprinkle them with powdered sugar, serve them with whipped cream or flame them with heated cognac or bourbon.

165

COEUR À LA CRÈME

serves 12

The true, classic French recipe for this dessert takes 24 hours to make and is what it says, "the heart of the cream." It is also ten times as rich as this which was developed by an American dairy products association. The molded cream is smooth and light, the sauce tart and fresh—a perfect summer dessert.

2 pints cottage cheese
2 cups commercial sour
  cream
¼ tsp salt

2 envelopes unflavored
  gelatin
½ cup milk
Strawberry-Orange Sauce
  (recipe follows)

In an electric blender, purée the cottage cheese, sour cream and salt together. Soften the gelatin in the milk and stir it in the top of a double boiler until completely dissolved. Blend with the cottage cheese mixture. A heart-shaped mold is the ideal but any other pretty shape will do. Rinse a 1½ quart mold with cold water and pour in the cheese mixture. Refrigerate, covered with plastic film, until firm. Unmold and serve the following sauce.

STRAWBERRY-ORANGE SAUCE

½ cup sugar
2 Tb cornstarch
¾ cup orange juice

¼ cup lemon juice
1 pint fresh strawberries
1 Tb grated lemon rind

Stir the sugar and cornstarch together in a small saucepan. Gradually stir in the orange and lemon juices and when blended, cook over medium low heat stirring constantly until thickened. Set aside. Reserve a few whole berries for garnish and slice the rest. Stir them into the sauce with the lemon rind. Refrigerate until serving time, then spoon a little over each serving of the Coeur à la Crème. The entire recipe can be made a day in advance if desired but the sauce is better if freshly made.

desserts

CHARLOTTE MARTINIQUE

serves 8 adults or 4 children

Right after Batman, on another channel, Julia Child demonstrates her French Chef techniques to the television audience. My husband, 4-year-old daughter and I watch both programs avidly. This is an adaptation of one of her recipes.

Line a charlotte mold with Italian ladyfingers cut in half lengthwise and dipped into a mixture of

> ½ cup rum
> ½ cup water
> 1 Tb sugar

Fill the mold with softened vanilla or butter pecan ice cream and chill in the freezer until firm. Unmold and drizzle ½ cup of melted semisweet chocolate bits over the top. Serve with or without whipped cream.

Note: Ice cream should never be rock hard. This dessert is easier to serve and nicer to eat if it is taken out of the freezer 10 or 15 minutes before serving.

MOUSSE CAFÉ

serves 12

An elegant, creamy dessert, beautiful to look at and sublimely soothing to food frustrations. It's very rich though it seems light as a cloud.

6 egg yolks
½ cup sugar
1¼ cups strong coffee

2 envelopes unflavored gelatin
½ cup cold water
1½ pints heavy cream

Beat the egg yolks with the sugar. Beat in the coffee and cook, stirring, over low heat until the mixture forms a thin custard. Off heat, stir in the gelatin which has been softened in ½ cup of cold water. Blend thoroughly and cool the custard. Whip the cream and fold it into the cooled custard. Rinse a 2-quart mold with cold water, pour in the mousse mixture and chill until firm. Unmold and serve with the following sauce.

SAUCE

This is a thin, transparent sauce that makes a rich, dark glaze on the pale coffee color of the mousse underneath.

⅔ cup sugar
1½ cups strong coffee
1½ Tb arrowroot flour or cornstarch
1 Tb cognac

Dissolve the sugar in the coffee over low heat. Mix the arrowroot or cornstarch with a few spoonfuls of water and the cognac. Stir into the sauce and cook until clear and thickened. The sauce will be quite thin but will thicken more when it is chilled.

desserts

FRESH PLUM PUDDING

serves 8

As a child, this is what I thought I was going to get when "Plum Pudding" was mentioned. It is just a glorified bread pudding and may also be made with peaches, cherries, apricots or blueberries.

8 to 10 red plums, pitted
    and sliced
10-12 slices day-old
    home-style bread
    butter
4 cups milk

5 eggs
¾ cup sugar
2 oz Cointreau
1 vanilla bean or 2 tsp vanilla
    extract
3 plums for decoration,
    pitted and sliced

Trim crusts from the bread and butter each slice. Cut into uniform cubes. Sprinkle the cut-up plums lightly with about 1 tablespoon of the sugar and mix well. Butter a large soufflé dish (3-quart capacity) and put in the bread cubes and plums, mixed. Sprinkle with Cointreau. Scald the milk with a vanilla bean and the remaining sugar. Remove the vanilla bean. Pour slowly, stirring constantly, over the well-beaten eggs. Pour this custard over the bread mixture. Rim the dish with overlapping plum slices. Bake at 350° F. for approximately 30 minutes (until a knife inserted in the center comes out clean). Serve with unsweetened whipped cream or plain.

INDEX